Developing a Championship Quarterback

John Bond

COACHES CHOICE ™

ISBN: 978-1-60679-351-0
Library of Congress Control Number: 2015960887
Cover design: Cheery Sugabo
Book layout: Cheery Sugabo
Front cover photo: Nelson Chenault-USA TODAY Sports

Coaches Choice
P.O. Box 1828
Monterey, CA 93942
www.coacheschoice.com

Dedication

I would like to dedicate this book to the most important people in my life. First of all, my mom and dad, Sara and Gary Bond, have been there every step of the way. No little boy or grown man has ever had any more loving and supportive parents than the two of you have been. I thank you, I appreciate you, and I love you.

To my wife Jenny, who for the last 15 years has celebrated championships, withstood firings, and endured the year-to-year uncertainty of this crazy business, I can't thank you enough. She has allowed me to be able to do my job, while wearing many hats. She has been the plumber, the electrician, the painter, the housekeeper, the accountant, and the cook. In addition to that, she has recently added school teacher to her long and arduous list. While doing all that, she is raising three wonderful children, who are all busy with activities of their own. You are the glue that holds things together, and for all of that, I love you and cannot possibly thank you enough.

Mackenzie, Mallory, and Brody, all three of you are the light of my life. Maybe one day, when all of you have kids of your own, you will truly understand how much your daddy loves you. I will love all of you forever.

Acknowledgments

I would like to thank David Lee, currently the quarterback coach of the Buffalo Bills, for giving me my first chance to coach the quarterbacks. Coach Lee hired me in 1991 to coach his quarterbacks at the University of Texas at El Paso. His curiosity and passion for coaching the mechanics of the position and the fundamentals of really how to throw the football rubbed off on me, and it's something I still carry with me today. Even back then, Coach Lee had 16 mm cutups of the greats of the 80s throwing the ball and all of the fundamental things they had in common. Nobody in the world, to my knowledge, studies the mechanics of throwing the football like David Lee. His extensive library of the most accurate passing quarterbacks in the world, which is large, encompasses through the 90s and up to the present day. Everything he taught me back then has been reinforced every day of every football season. The mechanics that are discussed in this book are more true to me today than they were 24 years ago. About 98 percent of the time when a quarterback misses a throw, the reason for the errant pass can be traced right back to the mechanics that are discussed in detail in this book.

I would like to thank my current boss, Jason Simpson at UT Martin, for allowing me the latitude to finish this book in the time that is running up on spring practice. He has done a great job as the head coach of the Skyhawks, and his blessing with this book is appreciated. I appreciate the assistance of Coach Jordan Hankins, also a member of the UTM staff, for his knowledge about the latest strength and conditioning trends. I would also like to thank Coach Ben Luther, currently the tight ends coach at UTM. Without his technical assistance and knowledge of computers, this book could have never been written. I would like to say a special thank you to Coach Justin Rascati, the Skyhawks wide receivers coach at UT Martin. He is a former national championship-winning quarterback at James Madison University and is truly a quarterback at heart. Every time I got stuck or didn't articulate something as well as I would like, he was able to help and even suggested a couple of chapters, because the additional material sounded like something he would be interested in reading. Justin is a future star in this business, and his help with the book is much appreciated, as is his friendship.

I would like to say thanks to every quarterback whom I've had the privilege to coach over the last 24 years. I probably learned just as much from all of you as you did from me. I enjoyed our time together, and I continue to get great satisfaction at watching all of you turn into great husbands, fathers, and leaders in your communities.

Finally, I would like to thank the good folks at Coaches Choice for their assistance with the editing and publishing of this book. I'd like to especially thank Leslie Butler for asking me to write this book. It has been a lot of fun.

Foreword

So …do you want to be really smart and captivating next football season? How cool would it be to interrupt one of the talking heads during your team's big game with something like, "This quarterback is a great faker. Watch him accelerate on his naked boot course, even though he has handed off already. That middle linebacker still has no idea where the ball is!" Your significant other and all the resident football junkies will be duly impressed. How can you ever hope to become an instant football expert? Read John Bond's book.

Oh, and if you are a quarterback coach and think you know all you need to know, you better read it too. John really knows his stuff.

John Bond is both interesting and engaging. In a world of simplistic, driven people, he is complex, constantly learning, and forever looking for new dimensions. He is a real "lifer" football coach, who understands the nuts and bolts of the quarterback position as well as anyone I know and can organize his thoughts, articulate his insights, and communicate essential information.

That's not all, however. John can write. His book on quarterback play captures many of the fascinating aspects of football, while offering detailed instructions on the most complicated position in all of sport. Bond's understanding of every detail and thought process of quarterback play virtually leaps off every page. Relatively unfamiliar quarterback skills, like ballhandling and coverage reads, become interesting and memorable to readers. Like all good writers, he helps the reader to see the process in action.

I am one of the luckiest former offensive centers in the history of the game. I was in the huddle with great quarterbacks most of my playing career, led by renowned football icons, such as Bart Starr and Johnny Unitas. I know what a quarterback looks like. I know how a quarterback thinks. So does John Bond.

—Bill Curry

Contents

Introduction

When Leslie Butler of Coaches Choice asked me to write this book, I was somewhat hesitant, because I was right in the middle of recruiting and was worried that I wouldn't have enough time to do the book justice. The more I thought about it, however, the more I became excited about writing this book because I think it is a story that needs to be told. All sorts of literature on quarterback play, as well as a few very popular books that have been published recently, exist that don't speak to the 99.9 percent of the quarterbacks out there who need to adhere to consistent mechanics to accurately throw the football.

In reality, there are a handful of quarterbacks in the world who can make any throw they want to make at any time. It doesn't matter where their feet are, where their shoulders are, or even where their arm slot is. These guys are so gifted that they can make consistently accurate throws and don't have to do the same thing twice.

In my opinion, some of the existing reading material on quarterback play talks way too much about several of the things these few men can do and tries to make it sound like that is what every other quarterback in the world should either do or possess in order to be a consistent passer. I believe that power, accuracy, and consistency come from the lower body—a factor that will be addressed at length in this book. This point has been demonstrated and proven to me every play of every day of practice over the course of the last 24 years that I have been coaching quarterbacks.

Not only do quarterbacks need a quarterback coach, they also need a concrete and consistent set of mechanics that can be referred to on every play. Think about it, if almost every great golfer in the world has a swing coach, who coaches the golfer on one of the most intricate and detailed movements in sport, then why would a quarterback on every competitive level not need a road map to have a consistent throwing motion and a constant set of quarterback mechanics?

When I go to clinics and listen to offensive coordinators or quarterback coaches, all they ever talk about are plays and schemes, as opposed to quarterback mechanics and fundamentals. Plays and schemes are overrated. It doesn't matter how intoxicating the latest and greatest scheme is, if the quarterback and his teammates don't have the necessary fundamentals and mechanics to properly execute those schemes, then those schematics are dead in the water. Every time I turn on the television or watch film, I see quarterbacks who could be better if they had more consistent mechanics, a group that includes quarterbacks who play in the National Football League.

Hopefully, this book will address some of the misinformation, if you will, that is out there and will also address virtually every fundamental that a quarterback needs to develop in order to become a championship quarterback. This book also covers several factors that are rarely talked about, like film study and the year-round process that quarterbacks need in order to become the best that they can become. Furthermore, this book reviews the process it takes to make a quarterback into a more consistently accurate passer. Make no mistake about it, the world is full of many high profile coaches, as well as a number of very highly paid quarterback tutors, who may have very differing opinions than the ones detailed in this book. I believe that the things that are discussed in this book are spot-on. Not only have I witnessed every day for the past 24 years how these mechanics work, I have also been in the trenches with these quarterbacks every day for that length of time.

The quarterback position is the most important position in all of team sports. It's also the most difficult to play. In today's brand of football, if a team doesn't have a good quarterback, that team can pretty much be assured that it isn't going to win a championship. It is my hope that everyone who reads this book can pick something up to help him make his quarterback better. Given that the quarterback is the individual who drives the train, I sincerely hope that this book can help quarterback coaches on every competitive level *develop a championship quarterback.*

CHAPTER 1
What a Championship Quarterback Looks Like

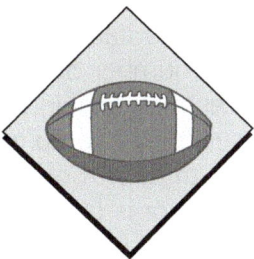

A set mold of what a championship quarterback looks like doesn't exist. Quarterbacks come in all sizes and shapes. There are tall ones and short ones. There are husky ones and skinny ones. There are fast ones and slow ones. You can't just go down to the stadium and say, "Yep, there he is! I'm going to start molding my championship quarterback, because this is what he is supposed to look like!" I've seen a bunch of great-looking specimens who couldn't play the quarterback position in any way, shape, or form.

A number of misconceptions exist about some of the characteristics that are necessary to play winning football at the quarterback position. The first one that is heard all of the time is that a quarterback has to be tall to play the position in order to see over the linemen in front of him. That is simply not the case. First of all, even if quarterbacks are 6'4", in most cases, they would still have to throw over a defensive lineman who is just as tall and has his hands up. That scenario would require him to be about seven and a half feet to nine feet tall. Obviously, that situation isn't going to happen.

Quarterbacks don't throw over people. They create throwing lanes by moving around in the pocket, so that they have a clear path to make the throw. Whether a quarterback is 5'9" or 6'4", there won't be many balls going over the outstretched hands of a defensive tackle, defensive end, or linebacker who has his hands up.

There have been a number of championship quarterbacks and even NFL Hall of Famers who weren't even six-feet tall. It's been pretty well-documented that in the history of the NFL, the overall numbers of the best 6'0" tall-and-under quarterbacks match up extremely well with the best quarterbacks who are 6'2" and above.

Another common misconception about quarterbacks is they must have a strong arm. In reality, several players exist who have a canon for an arm and can't hit the broad side of a barn on a consistent basis. While arm strength is nice, it is not essential in having a great quarterback. Even when quarterbacks throw takeoff or go routes, the ball is seldom in the air more than 50 yards. Even those types of routes have more to do with timing, than they do with arm strength. Timing, anticipation, ball placement, and the ability to see clearly when everything is caving in are way more important than arm strength.

All too often, guys with strong arms have only one pitch, a fastball. Fastballs aren't always easy to catch, especially at short distances and with defenders breathing down their necks. Furthermore, there are a number of quarterbacks who have strong arms, who will try to force balls into places they shouldn't, because of the confidence they have in their arm strength. As a result, they end up turning the ball over more than the individual with lesser velocity on his throws. A quarterback with a strong arm, who is late throwing an out route to the field or is late on a curl route, because he doesn't have a feel for the timing of the throw, is a much bigger detriment than a player who has an OK arm, but has a great feel for the route, as well as the passing game in general, and throws the ball on time.

What about the quarterback who is fast? Coach Bill Curry played center for Johnny Unitas with the Baltimore Colts. He was voted the best player in the first 50 years of the NFL. I asked Coach Curry one day how fast did Unitas run the 40-yard dash. Coach said the fastest he ever saw him run a 40 was 5.5. That's slow even for an offensive lineman.

Rarely does a quarterback need to be fast or even lightning quick. What he needs to be if he is asked to run in today's spread offenses is savvy enough to get his offense five or six yards, when he does pull the ball, to keep the defense honest. If he is blessed enough to be fast and run farther than that, that attribute is icing on the cake, but it is certainly not a prerequisite for greatness. Speed has very little to do with all the things that a quarterback is asked to do to play championship football.

In reality, all quarterback coaches have their personal beliefs concerning what exactly are the common characteristics that all the great ones have. Certainly, everything that I believe is based on coaching, watching, teaching, and learning over the years. It is also based on having a balanced, two-prong offensive attack. While some of these traits could be debatable, based on everything I have witnessed over the years, the five characteristics that are absolutely crucial in what a championship quarterback possesses are the following:

- Accuracy
- Decision-making
- Toughness

- Competitiveness
- Leadership

Make no mistake about it, if the quarterback is not an accurate passer, there is no passing game. There certainly isn't a consistent passing game. Back in the old days, a team could be one-dimensional and either run it well or throw it well and still have an opportunity to win big. In football today, however, with all the multiplicity on the defensive side of the ball, it's hard to be one-dimensional. If a team doesn't throw the ball with consistency, they better be able to run the ball versus nine defenders down, all of them within seven yards of the ball, because that's exactly what they are going to get.

With the exception of the wishbone (and there are only a couple of advocates left out there), teams have to be good at both running and throwing the ball to be able to compete for a championship. A huge component of that requirement is being able to consistently throw the football to move the chains and score points in the process. A great passing attack is one that is able to throw the ball effectively on first, second, and third down. In order to do that, the football team needs an accurate quarterback. Again, back in the old days, if the quarterback threw for 50 percent, teams were doing just fine. In contrast today, teams better complete at least 65 percent of their passes, or they won't be able to sustain drives like the champions are able to sustain drives. The quarterback must throw completions.

Accuracy has nothing to do with arm strength. Rather, it has to do with being able to put the ball where the quarterback wants to put the ball and when he wants to put the ball there the vast majority of the time. Again, arm strength is not mentioned. Arm strength and accuracy are not synonymous a lot of times. The most accurate passers have the best mechanics and, even more importantly, the most consistent mechanics about 99 percent of the time.

The NFL has a few quarterbacks who can get away with poor mechanics and poor footwork because of their extreme talent. In fact, a couple of NFL quarterbacks exist who can throw completions and never do anything the same way twice.

Consistent mechanics for the quarterback are kind of like free-throw shooting for a basketball player. When a basketball player goes to the free-throw line, he has a set number of dribbles every time. He may spin the ball. He might want the logo of the ball facing him.

Whatever his routine is, that is what the great quarterbacks have when they are throwing the football. Their feet are the same every time, unless they are under duress. Their release is the same most every time, unless they are throwing around a defender or are under duress and have to change their release point.

The most accurate quarterbacks are also the most consistent quarterbacks, when it comes to the mechanics of throwing the football. Accurate passers must first practice accuracy. This focus should start every day, when they're warming up. Quarterbacks should never warm up without having a buddy who gives them a target every time. Accurate quarterbacks take pride in being able to put the ball where they want it. They take pride in practicing putting the ball on the numbers of the receiver away from the defender. They practice throwing the ball on an out route, where only the receiver can catch it. Accuracy can and must be practiced. Unless your quarterback can consistently deliver the ball to the right guy, at the right time, and under duress, your pass game offense will struggle to consistently be able to move the football.

The ability to be able to process a ton of information in an unbelievably short amount of time and be able to make the right decisions is crucial. This factor as much as any of the five musts for a quarterback, separate the good ones from the great ones. The amount of information is so vast concerning what a championship quarterback has to know before the ball is even snapped is amazing.

There have been a number of good high school quarterbacks who come to college and think they can just roll out to practice without working at their game. At some point in every quarterback's development, the playing field levels out. The players become bigger, faster, and stronger. Eventually, they can't get by just on natural ability alone. The players who become great at the level of their next challenge sometimes have to learn to reinvent themselves a little bit. What got them by before won't necessarily get them by on the next step. What made them stand out before won't necessarily make them stand out now.

Before every ballgame, a championship quarterback must master a checklist, if you will, that encompasses what he is about to encounter. The quarterback obviously must have a complete knowledge of the offense inside and out. He must know what every man on his team does on every single play.

The quarterback must also understand the front and coverage structure of the defense he is about to face. In addition, he must have a great grasp of the defensive personnel he is about to play. Who is their best defensive lineman, linebacker, and defensive back? Who is he going to try to take advantage of? What must he do in order to neutralize their best players? What defensive back is he going to try and take advantage of? Which plays have problems versus certain defensive fronts? What are the blitz checks? What looks force a change in the pass protections? The quarterback must know all of the aforementioned things in order to have his best chance for being successful.

On every play, the quarterback must also know what the down and distance for a first down is. How much time is left? What is the score? Where is his team on the field? Does he need to speed up or slow down? He has to understand what the objectives of his coaches are for this particular drive.

He has to always know every single time where he is relative to the 40-second clock. Delay-of-game penalties and wasted timeouts are a sign of bad coaching, as well as bad quarterback play. These types of errors make teams look bad and can even get good teams beat. All of these factors have to be known before a play is even executed. All of these things play into his decision-making. As before, he needs to know and consider these factors before a ball is even snapped.

If the quarterback has a good grasp of all of the aforementioned situations and scenarios, he can then start to deal with the play itself. Are the defenders' body postures looking like they are playing base defense or do they have the posture of a possible blitz? These observations, which can be ascertained by a lot of film study, are of crucial importance in the decision-making process.

He must be able to determine the aforementioned, in some cases, in less than a couple of seconds and then decide whether to keep the play or check the play to something else. If a pass play is called, is the secondary rotating coverage? If so, what and how does that change his read or progression? Are the eyes of the corner on the receiver, indicating man coverage, or are his eyes in the backfield indicating zone? All of this information has to be processed in milliseconds. As such, the ability to process the information and arrive at the right decisions can make all the difference in a good quarterback, a bad quarterback, or a great quarterback.

I've never been around a great quarterback who wasn't tough. If the goal of the coaching staff is to win a championship, the quarterback better be the toughest son of a gun on the team. A championship quarterback must have the guts to stand in there and get hit in his teeth and yet get up and go again. The quarterback must have the guts to set his feet every time, knowing he is going to take a shot. That scenario is a huge component of toughness.

Over the years, it has also been determined that toughness encompasses more than just the physical aspect. There is the mental aspect of toughness as well. The great ones have the ability to be at their best when their best is needed. A big part of the ability to be at your best, when your best is needed, has a great deal to do with the quarterback being able to not let anything be a distraction to him at that particular moment. He needs to be in the moment and to focus on the job at hand.

How many Super Bowls achieved legendary status, because the quarterback was mentally tough enough to focus on the job at hand and take his team down the field on a drive to win the game? How many national championships and conference championships have been won, because the guy in charge of the drive was tough enough mentally to get his team down the field and score?

A quarterback's ability to be tough enough to handle any coaching he receives is also important. Can he take the criticism that comes with the position from his coach? Is he going to go into a shell and pout, or is he going to shake it off and come back and execute the next play? How your quarterback reacts to getting coached is very important, because everybody on your team is watching how he handles it and will play off of it accordingly. Having a quarterback who is coachable goes a long way in having a very coachable team. A championship quarterback has the mental toughness it takes to be coached and be positive about it. His teammates will look at him and how he handles tough situations. A championship quarterback will find a way to get it done.

Another component of mental toughness is being able to handle the criticism of the media and fans. There has been many a quarterback who melted when the media started blaming him for a loss, or the fans booed him because he made a bad play or played poorly in a game. A great quarterback tunes all that out and goes about the business of getting better each day. In the current age of social media, it is better if both coaches and players alike don't read the newspapers, twitter, or Facebook, or even watch the television. In reality, a lot of negativity exists that essentially serves no purpose. As such, the expression that it is poison to listen to either all the good or all the bad that is said or written could not be more true in the times in which we live. The most mentally tough quarterbacks shake all negative distractions off and go back to work.

Locker rooms aren't always the greatest places in the world to be, if an athlete has thin skin. The public often hears about the practical jokes, the laughing, and the horseplay that occur in locker rooms. In reality, the locker room can sometimes be a hard place to be when teammates are critical or the quarterback hears someone saying something that isn't the most flattering thing in the world. A championship quarterback knows that as part of his job description he must take the criticism from the coaches, the fans, the media, and even his teammates.

The head coach and the quarterback are the two most focal points of a football team. As such, they both have to know that with all the attention they are going to get, not all of it is going to be positive. The exceptional ones are able to shake off criticism from their teammates and move on. That is a part of being in a leadership role. Great leaders take the blame, even when they and everyone else knows it wasn't their fault.

The quarterback position is the most demanding position in all of sports. It is also the most scrutinized, talked about, and written about position in all of sports. The ability to focus on the job at hand on a daily basis is what the great ones do. The ability to compartmentalize the things that happen during a practice or a game makes all the difference in the world. The old saying "play the next play" is absolutely true. Whether it is a great play or a bad play, the championship quarterbacks go to the next play to the very best of their ability. The quarterbacks who are able to do that are usually the individuals who figure out a way to win.

I've never been around a great quarterback who wasn't the most competitive person in the room. He wants to win at everything and won't stop until he does. It doesn't matter if it's pitching horseshoes, playing pool or ping pong, or shooting a game of horse in the backyard, if it's a game, and there is competition, he wants to beat everyone. A great quarterback will never settle for second place. He will compete until he wins.

This factor carries over to every aspect of a quarterback's preparation for a game. He will want to learn his opponent better than any other athlete in the room, including the other quarterbacks. He will take pride in seeing something on the tape that nobody else saw. He will then take that knowledge out to the practice field and hit more targets warming up than his fellow quarterbacks do. When individual drills start, he will want to do them more perfectly and better than everyone else in his group. When it comes time for the team to come together and practice, he will do everything he can to make sure his offense whips the defense every time, and if they don't, he will be ticked off.

A championship quarterback usually stays after practice after everyone else is gone to work on something he didn't do as well as he wanted to. More often than not, these athletes are most always the first ones out to practice and the last ones to leave. The point to remember is that the value of a great competitor should never be underestimated.

The aforementioned brings to mind a story about one of my quarterbacks at Army. Chad Jenkins, who was maybe 5'11", weighed 175 pounds soaking wet. He was going into his junior year, when our staff got to Army in late December. In fact, he was one of the first people I met. He was one of those guys who, every time you looked up, he was under your feet. I could tell how excited he was to compete for the starting job.

The cadet whom he was competing against was an individual by the name of Joe Gerena. Joe was a tough kid and a good player. He had started for years and was the hero of the Army-Navy game the year before. Joe wanted to start too. As such, both of those guys meant business when it came to competing for that job. I was new, so I could justify the open competition, since we were changing offenses and hadn't seen either of them play or practice live.

They both competed and had good springs. Subsequently, I told both of them how important that summer was for their preparation and competition for the starting job. I also informed them that I didn't want to play two quarterbacks. I only wanted to play one. Not surprisingly, they both went to work.

Both of them came back in great shape. Fall camp started off just like in the spring. Every rep was like the Super Bowl. Both kids were killing themselves for that starting job. One day late in training camp, we were off by ourselves, just the quarterbacks and me, working on footwork drills and drops.

I saw Chad was acting a little weird, and I asked him what was wrong. He said he had to go pee. I told him to go ahead and go to the bathroom. Our individual area was right by the tunnel, leading out into the stadium and right by a bathroom. He said no, he was good to go. I never thought anything about it, but the next thing you know, instead of missing one almost insignificant rep in an individual drill, he peed down the leg of his football pants. You think football wasn't important to that kid?

You think I wouldn't trust our offense with him? You think when he did four tours in Iraq and Afghanistan that I didn't sleep better at night, knowing he was over there protecting our freedom? Needless to say, after a hard competition, Chad became our starter and, in 2001, became the hero of the Army-Navy game, because he played the game on one leg, with torn knee ligaments. He is still the last Army quarterback to beat Navy.

Finally, the championship quarterbacks are great leaders. Being a great leader starts with being a great follower, which entails being completely coachable. A coachable athlete continuously gives great effort, exhibits exceptional intensity, shows noteworthy concentration, and focuses his attention on the task at hand. I've always felt that the quarterback can be "one of the boys" until he walks into the meeting room or on the practice field. At that point, the separation begins. If everyone sees how locked in the quarterback is, at all times, they will see and understand how important doing whatever is necessary to win is to him. That's where the leadership starts to show itself. Once that happens, your quarterback can start moving his teammates in the direction he desires them to go.

Being a great leader also involves the quarterback showing his teammates how important they are. A great leader lets his teammates know there is no way this can be done as well as it needs to be done without them and their best effort. Not only do exceptional leaders heap substantial praise on others, they also seek out chances to praise their teammates. Anytime they get the chance, they will state how great the line blocked or how well their receivers caught the ball. Great leadership demands that the quarterback takes responsibility when things don't go his way and heaps lots of praise on everyone else when they do go well.

Great leaders demand more of themselves than they do of others. Just because the quarterback may want to stay out late on the practice field to get some more work in doesn't mean that a great leader will expect the whole squad to stay out there with him. Just because he comes in an hour before everyone else to watch the film doesn't mean he expects everyone to sit in the video room with him. Without question, his teammates are always watching him. Because they will see the extra time he puts in, they will further understand how important that the team plays well is to him. All factors considered, it becomes easy to follow someone who cares so much.

Being a great leader means that the quarterback will exhibit leadership both on and off the field. He can be one of the boys off the field. He can laugh, cut-up, play jokes, and have a great time with the guys, but he will also be an individual who isn't doing something that isn't supposed to be done. He won't break the team's training rules. He will encourage his buddies to do what is right where the team is concerned. He will be the person to pull someone out of a bad situation. He will be the individual who will drive someone home when they need help. He will be the one who says it's time to go home, when it's time to go home, according to the training rules set by the coaching staff.

Is it possible to be a great leader and not be a vocal leader? I guess it's possible, but I haven't seen many great quarterbacks who weren't vocal leaders. Does that mean screaming and cussing and waving your arms when the quarterback wants something done or something doesn't go right? Of course, it doesn't. You can be a vocal leader by being an encourager. You can be a vocal leader by standing up and saying there is not enough effort being put in the weight room or on the practice field. It could entail telling a receiver he cut his route off by two yards, which was why the ball sailed two yards over his head. A leader by example is a dime a dozen. In contrast, a vocal leader is priceless.

Can a team have a championship quarterback without one or even several of the characteristics that have been addressed in this chapter? I guess there have been, but the vast majority of the great ones, at a minimum, possess some or all of these five components. A few of the five are just they either have it or they don't. It's difficult to teach toughness. It's hard to teach someone to be competitive. On the other hand, it is possible to help someone understand what it takes to be a great leader.

In reality, coaches can enhance the leadership skills of their quarterback. In fact, it's done every day by a number of very good coaches. Many coaches, for example, to try at least once a week in the off-season to talk about the array of different aspects of leadership, e.g., how a championship quarterback works in the weight room in front of his teammates in the winter months after the season. It can also be beneficial for a coach to express to his quarterback the expectation and value of him finishing first in all of the running drills. In addition, it would be very constructive for a coach to tell his quarterback how his teammates need to see him watching film and asking them to go throw on a pretty day.

A checklist needs to be made every off-season to tailor the leadership training to the particular person or group. In that regard, it's a great idea for all quarterback coaches to help their guys along who aren't quite where they need to be with their leadership skills. In reality, such an attitude is good for the whole team. It should also be noted that there are many ways to help a young man with his accuracy in throwing a football, a subject that will be addressed in detail in later chapters.

In reality, what a championship quarterback looks like has very little to do with what he looks like and a whole lot more to do with who he is. Is he an accurate passer? Can he process information quickly? Is he mentally and physically tough? Is he competitive as all get out and is he a leader? If the answer is yes, then the football team has a viable opportunity to win a whole bunch of games.

CHAPTER 2
Intangibles

Every quarterback brings something different to the table in terms of his intangibles. Some of these attributes can be coached and enhanced, while others are just inherent to that particular kid. One intangible that separates the good ones from the great ones is the ability to see the field. The ability to see and have a great feel for what is happening is kind of like the great chess players who can see the entire board, anticipate his opponent's next move, and be two steps ahead.

The same situation exists with a great quarterback. Not only does he have to be able to see the route his wide receiver or running back is running, he also has to be able to see the defenders and how they are aligned. He has to be able to see and feel the direction to which they are leaning or moving. He has to understand the defensive structure and anticipate what the defenders are getting ready to do.

Not all quarterbacks can do that. Most good quarterbacks can do some of it. Most really good quarterbacks can see most of it, but not all of it. The great ones can see it like it's moving in slow motion. The great ones can see it and can anticipate where and when the ball needs to be thrown.

In reality, the great quarterbacks rarely throw the ball to an open receiver in zone coverage. Rather, they throw the ball to an open area or a window, if you will. The championship quarterback can see the route, see the defenders, and let the ball go,

s out of his break. Mind you, all of these steps
ng loose around the quarterback. Big bodies are
s big men who are trying to protect him.

ers are coming with bad intentions. The great
omeone coming after them. Their concentration
coming toward them. They are totally locked in
or progression is for that particular play.

s rush or the defender. They feel the pass rush
ive themselves an open throwing lane, which is,
In reality, very few people can do that.

rmchair quarterbacks have all the answers when
television. Until someone stands back there and
ppreciation for how daunting it can be. It's very
eople can do it. To stand in there, throw the ball,
and get hit right in the mouth by a 300 pound defensive tackle who is running full speed takes a special person. The ability to focus and to truly be able to see and anticipate, while manipulating defenders with his eyes and actions, takes a very courageous person. The challenge that the quarterback faces is further complicated by the fact that the gift of being able to truly see the entire field in such a situation is very rare.

I've set up drills where I station defenders in a certain area and have a receiver run his route and make the quarterback throw the ball to an open area. I have tried to set it up to help the quarterback's anticipation and feel of the play and force-feed him into this concept. Usually, the quarterbacks succeed at the drill, but in actual game conditions, if your quarterback doesn't have great vision and great anticipation, he will revert back to what and who he is. As a result, that ball may not get thrown, whereupon he may go to his next progression.

The ability to be able to see is innate and very difficult to coach. In fact, very few quarterbacks have this gift, which is why it is the number one intangible for a championship quarterback. If you have an athlete who can see and has a great feel for action on the field and can anticipate, you have the makings of a championship quarterback.

The next intangible that I absolutely love is the quarterback to be a "gym rat." He has to be a player who loves the game. He can't get enough of it. Every time you look up, he's under your feet wanting to watch tape, talk ball, or go throw to his buddies. Every great quarterback loves to throw. It's kind of like the basketball player who loves to go shoot baskets. He will go outside by himself and shoot for hours.

The same factor is true for a "gym rat." Anytime he has some free time, he is looking for someone who will catch for him. His teammates will feed off of this attitude, which helps enhance his position as a team leader. His enthusiasm for the game will be contagious for his team.

A "gym rat" will wear you out wanting to watch film. He will be there before you get to work, he will come over his lunch hour, and he will show up about the time you are trying to go home and see your family. These film sessions, in which the standard installation of a game plan or practice film is not being undertaken, are often the most productive times between you and your quarterback. All factors considered, these film sessions, on occasion, can be a little less professional and a whole lot more relaxed.

I can't tell you the number of times that something will come up, while watching film, which would have never been covered in a conventional quarterback meeting. In reality, there are so many variables that are associated with playing the quarterback position that it is absolutely impossible to cover them all. When you think you've covered them all, 10 more will pop up in the blink of an eye.

Another factor that often occurs during your early morning or late-night film session is that you both will start knowing what the other person is thinking. The bond between the two of you becomes stronger during these sessions than at any other time. He will know what you are thinking, and you will come to understand what he is thinking. The next time you send a play in, he will know exactly what is going through your head. For example, if you call a play, and he misses the throw or misses the read or opportunity, and you come right back to it and call the same play again, he will know why. More often than not, he will then execute it to perfection. This situation will occur because of the extra time you have spent together and the understanding that has been gained because of it.

A "gym rat" generally is the closest thing there is to having another coach on the field. He is just like you, because he loves ball, just like you. Having a "gym rat" for a quarterback makes it better for you and his teammates, because he is putting in a coach's hours. As a result, his feel and understanding is so much better than his teammates, and his love for the game is so obvious that it enhances his status as a leader of the team. In reality, the value of a "gym rat" who is your quarterback is incalculable.

Poise is hard to define, but easy to see in the heat of battle. Poise is the ability to keep your focus, while others around you are losing theirs. It's easy to be a poised quarterback when things are going well. What about when you are getting your butt beat, and the fans are starting to boo? What about when you feel like the referees have missed at least three calls in a row, and the people in the stands and your teammates are losing their minds? Those circumstances are examples of situations where a poised leader and a poised quarterback can come in handy.

It's hard to think straight, if you aren't a poised person. It's difficult to make good decisions when you are not in a poised frame of mind. Great quarterbacks have to make sound decisions in the worst of circumstances. If a quarterback doesn't have poise, his chances of making great decisions are not very good.

Poised quarterbacks are able to handle the highs and lows during the course of a game and the course of a season. Poised quarterbacks know that during every game, there is going to be adversity and challenges. Poised quarterbacks know the only way to ride the wave through adversity is to be able to play the next play to the best of their ability. A great quarterback handles a bad play or bad series just like he handles a great play or a touchdown drive. He plays the next play, with a calm and cool head.

Poised quarterbacks know that part of playing the next play to the best of their ability is employing the fundamentals that they were taught. Having great poise involves going back to the basics on each and every play. If a quarterback has missed his last five throws in a row, for example, how does he throw that next one for a completion? He knows he must get his feet right and set up exactly where the coach told him to so he can do his job. Anytime adversity exists, a poised quarterback knows to make sure he is executing the fundamentals of his position.

On occasion, when a team starts to lose, they lose their discipline. The wide receiver doesn't run his route at the proper depth. The running back doesn't carry the ball high and tight or aims for the inside leg of a defender instead of the outside leg on a pass protection. All of those factors can add up, which is when the lack of execution for an offensive team shows up.

A championship quarterback who has poise can get his team back on track. As such he can his teammates to focus and pay attention to details. As a result, the offense starts moving the football again and scoring points. Not only can a poised quarterback keep himself in the right frame of mind, he can also keep his teammates where they need to be from an emotional standpoint. A poised quarterback affects an entire squad, just like a quarterback who doesn't have poise can. An entire team will fall apart faster with a lack of poise at quarterback than it will at any other position. If your quarterback loses it, you need to get ready; you are headed downhill fast.

Fortunately, poise is something that can be taught to a certain extent. Have you ever seen a sideline where the coaches are yelling, screaming, and waving their arms, and the area looks like a total fire drill? How is it possible to ask your quarterback, the supposed leader of your team, to have any poise when that is going on? As such, poise is something that should be demonstrated by the coaches. Emotional composure is something that can be learned. Remember, it's hard to think clearly, if you don't have a clear head. Furthermore, it's hard to have a clear head, when you are losing your mind as a coach. Usually, the most successful coaches are those who are calm, cool, and collected. The same factor is true with the quarterback. The quarterbacks who keep their head about them when everyone else is losing theirs are the ones who are going to have way more success over the long haul than those who don't.

Great quarterbacks are like jet fighter pilots. They are confident. In fact, they are sometimes confident to the point of cockiness. I've never been around a great quarterback who wasn't a little cocky. The reason so many great quarterbacks have so much confidence is that they have been very successful in whatever they have done in life and just know they can do whatever it is they want to do. Confidence is gained by really only one factor—

demonstrated ability. You can't dream up confidence. You can't make it up. You have to do it. The great ones have done it and believe they can do it every time.

A huge part of confidence is how a great quarterback practices. I tell our quarterbacks that every rep is a game rep. You must put yourself in game mode on every play. If you have mentally put yourself in a game situation every rep, all week, those hundreds of reps add up. If on every drop, you have simulated how you will do it in the game, or on every throw you have made all week, the game should be easy. There should be very little nervousness because you are prepared. If you are prepared, there is no reason to be overly nervous.

You should be excited to perform but not extremely nervous. I remember as a player, I used to get so nervous. I was so worried about living up to expectations and playing great that I actually threw up before some games. That is ridiculous. I wish I could have those times back. If I could, I would have realized then that because I had practiced hard that week, I was ready to play and play well.

You have to make your quarterback understand that his preparation should lead to great confidence, not great nervousness. He needs to understand that it is crucial to be at game-speed on every rep. If he is totally locked in all day, every day, he will play with great confidence. This factor applies to the film room as well. If he prepares hard, watches the film hard, and doesn't just go through the motions of watching film, he will better know his opponent. He will also better understand the game plan. When he practices like he should, he will realize that there is no way he is not going to play great.

All of the great quarterbacks I've ever been around have been way more excited to play and perform than they were nervous. Nerves hinder you. They make you question and overanalyze. If the quarterback has worked like a championship quarterback is supposed to work during the week, he should have great confidence, as well as an attitude of anticipating success, when he takes the field.

Another reason why championship quarterbacks have great confidence is that they take great comfort in knowing that they have a complete knowledge of their own offense and the game plan, as well as knowing how his coach wants him to attack the other team. It's easy to be confident when you know what you are doing. When you combine knowing your own offense inside out, knowing the game plan inside out, and approaching every film session and practice rep as it they're game-like, how can you not feel like you can whip the world? Confidence is the key. People are attracted to and inspired by confidence. Great preparation leads to great confidence. Great confidence leads to victory.

The value of energy should never be underestimated. Energy is contagious as well. Energy gives people a reason to believe. People have great energy, when they love what they do. Everyone wants to be around an energetic person. Energy can give people a reason to finish practice. Energy can provide people with that extra little spark to make them finish the drill. Energy can make everyone have a little more fun, even in the most dreary of times. Usually, a high-energy person is a confident person. Energy, even if it's false energy, at times, can pick an entire team up during a bad practice or a bad game. It can be the force that stops the skid of a losing streak and helps turn the situation around.

As detailed in this chapter, the five intangibles that characterize every championship quarterback are his ability to see and anticipate, having a "gym rat" mentality, poise, confidence, and high energy. Those are my favorite intangibles.

Quarterbacks are different. Everyone is different and unique in his own way. It is important that a coach identifies what it is exactly his quarterback brings to the table. What does he bring and what does he not bring? What can the coach help him with and what does the quarterback absolutely not possess?

In my opinion, the ability to see and anticipate is God-given. On occasion, you may be able to enhance it a little, but the great ones just have it. I certainly believe that you can encourage your quarterback to try to be more aware of what's going on around him. On the other hand, if it's something that's not in his heart, as a rule, he is just watching film, not studying it. He is just throwing the ball around and will leave the first chance he gets.

You surely can teach poise or emotional composure by how you behave and who you are, especially in the heat of battle. If you are a good example, I think of all the five traits that are essential to championship quarterback play, this attribute is the one that a coach can most likely enhance.

Confidence is a more challenging factor. A quarterback can either do it, or he can't. He's either done it before, or he hasn't. It's demonstrated ability. It is impossible to dream up confidence.

Energy, on the other hand, is a factor that the quarterback can work on. It is important to note, however, that the energy a quarterback exhibits should be genuine, not false. If it's trumped up, it will be seen for what it is—phony.

There are other qualities of a championship quarterback that I could have noted. Making the right choices, having a positive attitude, handling your business, and having a great work ethic are all very important and are all worth mentioning. In this case, I chose to talk about my five favorite intangibles.

What a coach must do is find out what his quarterback has and do his best to help enhance whatever positive qualities he has. That is why he is called "coach." It's his job to figure out what his signal caller can do, and then mold his offense around him.

More than ever before, it's a quarterback-driven game now. A great coach will play to the strengths of his quarterback. The same factor applies to the quarterback's intangibles. It is the coach's responsibility to help cultivate the quarterback and hopefully be able to mold him into what he needs to be, not only on but off the field also. In today's game, whether it's Pop Warner ball all the way to the NFL, if a team doesn't have a productive quarterback, it won't be winning a championship.

CHAPTER 3
Relationship With Your Quarterback

One of the most important things to know about the relationship between the quarterback coach and the quarterback is that it differs from every other player on the team. Honestly, at times, the two individuals are more like peers than player and coach. Obviously, as his positon coach, you can't and shouldn't want to be buddies. That situation does not work.

Separation between player and coach always has to exist. A head coach and a quarterback coach's success is so tied into the quarterback and the time that you spend with one another is so great, however, that it's almost like you are going on the journey every day together. The quarterback has to see the game through your eyes, and you have to see it through his. You have to know exactly what he saw in order to be able to help him. He has to know what you saw and be able to understand what you're talking about.

The two of you are tied at the hip, almost like being married. You certainly spend more time with your quarterback during the season than you do your own wife. Because of all the time you spend together, given that you are both striving hard for the same goal, your relationship with him is different than what you have with everyone else.

Make no mistake about it, the relationship between the quarterback and his quarterback coach is the most important relationship on the entire team. If there is friction, animosity, or a lack of trust by either party, it's extremely difficult to have continued long-term success. I've always believed that mutual trust is the biggest factor in having a great relationship with your quarterback.

The quarterback has to know that you have his best interest at heart. He has to know that you care about him as a person and not just as a player. I've always gone out of my way to talk to quarterbacks about everything but football every chance I got. It might be about his parents, his girlfriend, school, or anything under the sun, but football.

When a coach does that, not only is he showing that he cares about him more than just as a player, you will get to know him on a much more personal level. You will actually come to know him as well or better than many of his friends and even some of his family. If a quarterback coach does it properly, he will have a relationship with his quarterback that will last a lifetime, because of the bonds made during their time together. I can honestly say that in all the years that I have been coaching quarterbacks, I can't think of more than a couple of kids with whom I don't stay in touch, who don't check in with me every so often. It is very gratifying. It is one of the best, if not the best, parts of my job.

Previously, the importance of establishing trust between the quarterback and his coach was discussed. One of the best ways to start establishing that trust factor is to start feeding little tidbits of information to your quarterback that you claim is top secret. While it may not really be top secret, you tell the quarterback that he can have access to it, if he will keep his word and not let the "secret" to get out. It might be about a player on your team. It might be about something that is going to come out in the media. Whatever it might be, it's important to see if he will keep the "secret" information to himself.

Such discretion is absolutely vital, because your quarterback has to know things that only the football staff knows, because he is an extension of you and your program. He has to be able to keep things to himself about personnel on the team during the course of a season that do not need to be known by other team members. It is very important that you are able to discuss whom you want to get the ball to on certain plays, and, in some cases, whom you don't want to get the ball. You have to talk about whom you want to run the ball behind in crunch time. On occasion, he may also have to know whom you don't want to run behind.

If the quarterback subsequently ran back in the locker room and told so-and-so that coach doesn't think he is any good and that he doesn't think that a particular player has the ability to do the job in every situation, you would have a big problem on your hands. The more you feel like you can trust what you are telling the quarterback, the deeper you can go into whatever information you'd like to tell him. You have to be able to discuss privately things like personnel, or even certain discipline situations, that may be coming down the pike, so that he can prepare mentally for this week's game, because someone may or may not be available. The possibilities are endless, with regard to what your quarterback may need to know in order for him to prepare to play winning football that next week.

The quarterback also has to feel that he can trust you with anything he tells you. He has to be comfortable enough to be able to share with you things that may be going on in his personal life. He has to be confident that he can confide in you about plays he may not like as much as you do or personnel he may not think is as good as you think. As the quarterback and leader of your team, he might feel like it's his duty to tell you about some team members who are breaking training or doing things they shouldn't be doing. Whatever the case may be, there has to be a great trust between both entities. Because of the deep bonds that are developed over time between a quarterback coach and his quarterback, the end result is usually a relationship that can last a lifetime.

Quarterbacks tend to be coached differently than other positions. While there are a few screamers and yellers out there who have had good success coaching quarterbacks, fortunately, they are few and far between. I've always felt that screaming and yelling at a quarterback is like the head coach screaming and yelling at his assistants. Although it may make the head coach feel better at the time, all it really does is mostly to have all of the players wondering what in the world is going on. Typically, it also makes the assistant coaches uneasy. Furthermore, the coach that's getting screamed at is thinking how can I do my job if he is going to embarrass me like that in front of my players?

In my opinion, a lot of times, coaches who scream, yell, and wave their arms at their quarterback make the other players on the squad wonder how in the world our team is going to be able to win the game, because our quarterback doesn't know what he is doing. I also think that such behavior takes away from the confidence of the unit as a whole.

It should be noted that no one is saying that a quarterback doesn't need his butt chewed every now and then. No one is claiming that he doesn't need to be disciplined when he is turning the ball over and making foolish decisions. As a coach, however, you need to pick and choose when and where you bark at him, as well as where you snap at him.

I am constantly snipping and coaching the quarterback on every single play. If I have to provide negative feedback, I generally try and deliver it discreetly, where not many individuals can hear what is being said. If it's positive, I want a whole bunch of people to hear what I have to say. Sometimes, if he throws the ball in a crowd and makes a decision in practice that can cost you a game, I might bark at him in front of his teammates or yank him out of the drill. For the most part, however, I try to instill confidence in the offense by not chewing him out in front of his teammates. If I am going to blister him, I will do it in the film room, only with his peers, and behind closed doors.

There are many ways to coach a quarterback. Is the aforementioned the best way? It is for me. It has worked for me. In my opinion, it's good for your quarterback to be coached like that. Furthermore, just as importantly, I think it's good for your offense, because if your players think their leader knows his stuff, it instills much more confidence doing it that way, than the other way around. This style of coaching your quarterback tends to make your relationship with him stronger, because he knows exactly what you are doing and why you are doing it, which tends to make him respect you all the more.

A big part of your relationship with your quarterback is managing expectations. His expectations, yours, the head coach's, the team's, and the general public's expectations have to be dealt with and managed. As has already been discussed, quarterbacks, especially the good ones, tend to be a confident bunch. How do you handle the quarterback who was demoted to the second team? How do you handle the psyche of a quarterback you had to bench? How do you keep your quarterback mentally up, when his head coach has lost confidence in him? How do you work the head coach behind the scenes to believe in your benched quarterback, if you still believe in him? How do you manage the quarterback who has just played the game of his life and his parents, friends, people at school, and media are making him out to be the next Joe Montana?

If you have done a good enough job establishing the trust in your relationship with your quarterback, and he knows you have his very best interests at heart, the best way to manage all of the expectations is to narrow it down to one issue. The only factor that should matter to him is he playing as well as he is capable? Is he meeting his own expectations, and is he meeting yours?

I tell quarterbacks all the time that the only two people I am trying to please are myself and the head coach, period. If you can break through all the junk, all the stuff going on around is just that. Is he pleasing himself, and is he pleasing me? If the answer is to either of both of those questions is no, then you have to figure out why.

It has already been established that neither you nor your quarterback are going to be reading the newspapers. You aren't going on twitter or the Internet, looking at anything good or bad being written or said. You should be doing your best to block out all of the distractions and make this situation as small as it is.

When you break the circumstances down like that, the situation becomes much more manageable. The hard part is where ego comes in. Everyone has an ego. I don't care how humble a person is; everyone has an ego. You can call it ego or pride, but we all have some form of it. When a kid is demoted to the second or third team, it's because he isn't playing as well as the player in front of him.

Part of coaching is being brutally honest with your athletes and telling them exactly why and what they need to do to get better. Some individuals handle it well, and some don't. Those who don't handle it well have to be taught how to handle adversity, because for some players, it may be the first time in their sporting life that they have faced it.

It doesn't matter who you are, at some point, the game is going to humble you. It's just like life. At some point, we all will be humbled. We all will fall short of expectations. Teaching a young person how to handle this situation is one of the most important things, as his coach, that you can teach him.

If he isn't playing as well as he can, the underlying objective should be to see if he can fix his shortcomings. If they can't be fixed, and he just flat out isn't as good as the people in front of him, that's when you earn your paycheck. I learned as a very young coach that the best way to be in this situation is brutally honest. If you believe a player isn't as good as whoever is in front of him, and he has no chance to be as good, you must tell him. Believe it or not, some of the young men I've had to do that to stay in touch, talk, and are as close to me as (or closer to me than) the individuals who played great. Deep down, most of these athletes know they aren't as good and deep down they appreciate your honesty.

If your quarterback knows that you have his back, he will be more willing to run through a wall for you. Sometimes, that occurs, when a difference of opinion exists between the head coach and you. The head coach may feel that another player gives the team a better chance to win than the quarterback coach does. Such a situation doesn't occur very often, but it happens. When it does, your quarterback needs to know that you will go in there and battle for him. He also has to know that ultimately, it's the head coach's decision.

If your relationship with your quarterback is what it should be, all he has to know is that you are with him and that you went to battle for him. As long as that happens, everything is OK. In reality, most quarterback and quarterback coach relationships are way stronger than quarterback and head coach relationships, because of all the factors that have been detailed in this chapter. Fundamentally, his expectation of you is to have his back, and if he knows you have his back, he will have yours.

How do you handle the quarterback who is playing out of his mind, and everyone is patting him on the back telling, him he is the greatest thing ever? Aside from a few unflattering jokes or maybe saying something a little crass or crude to him to let him know who is still the boss, the factor you always want to come back to is to have him focus on the task at hand. How is he going to play his best this play, this drive, this half, and this game?

Eliminate all the distractions, and break the situation down to its most basic form. Over the years, I've had multiple quarterbacks go a hundred or so throws in a row without throwing an interception. That level of performance is achieved by a basic, simple formula. Plan, prepare, and practice every rep like it's a game rep, and then go play. If your relationship is good with your quarterback, it shouldn't take very much to kiddingly knock him down a notch or two early in the week, if you feel he is starting to believe everything that he is hearing. More likely than not, he will understand what you are doing and will get back to business.

This player-coach relationship is one of the most challenging, but rewarding, aspects of your job. You will spend more time with him than you do your own family. You have to be his biggest cheerleader, as well as his biggest critic. You have to know when to get after him and when he needs to be stroked. All of this should be learned as it pertains to each individual player, because they are all different.

The more effort you put into the player, the deeper the impact you will have on him as a person and as a player. The trick is to be almost as close as brothers, and yet never lose the player-coach dynamic. You have to be able to put the hammer down at times, and he has to understand that. That separation has to exist, because, on occasion, tough decisions have to be made that aren't easy for anyone to make, let alone follow through on.

He has to know that you will be there for him no matter how rough or bad the situation is. He also has to know that you will do what it takes to win, including sitting him on the bench, if it is appropriate. If he knows that from the start of your relationship with him, the mutual respect level will take flight at that moment.

CHAPTER 4
How to Throw With Power, Accuracy, and Consistency

When I go to coaching clinics, all I tend to hear from quarterback coaches or offensive coordinators is everything under the sun, except the mechanics of how to play the position. The speakers will stand up and talk about how to execute the latest great route or a new way to block the jet sweep, but nobody ever talks about how to play the position of quarterback.

I once asked a very high profile NFL offensive coordinator what he thought about teaching the fundamentals of quarterback play and was their mini-camps the time in which he coached them. He told me that he didn't coach or even talk about fundamentals. He said if his quarterbacks didn't have the necessary fundamentals, he would go get someone else. I actually heard similar comments from another very high profile Super Bowl-winning offensive coordinator years earlier, when I asked him what footwork drills he would recommend for a slow-footed quarterback. He snapped back that he didn't know and didn't do footwork drills.

A couple of quarterback coaches that I personally know who do coach in the NFL tell me that even at that level, players—professional quarterbacks—are starving to be coached on the fundamental aspects of throwing the football better, as well as with more consistency. No one ever talks about how to throw the football with power, accuracy, and consistency.

When I do hear some coaches talk about the mechanics of throwing the football, I cringe at how crazy some of what they say sounds. It would be almost laughable, if it weren't so bad, that the most important position in all of sports has as much existing misinformation. This chapter addresses the essentials of throwing the football with power, accuracy, and consistency. I strongly believe in the information presented in this chapter. For one reason, I've studied and watched closely everything that I teach. In the process, I have seen this information hold up on every play of every practice of every season. It ties in when I watch major league pitchers and closely watch the mechanics of their pitching motion. It ties in to other sports, when you start talking about how to generate power, shift an athlete's weight, and follow through.

One of the reasons that I'm somewhat different than a lot of quarterback coaches and offensive coordinators is I undoubtedly get more of a kick out of coaching and teaching the fundamentals of the position than I do talking about scheme. I also am more interested in figuring out what makes a player tick and how can I motivate this athlete or offensive unit more than I do talking about the schematics of a particular play. While I believe that schemes are overrated, I don't think people are.

The Mechanics of How to Effectively Throw the Football

❑ A wide base. Power and accuracy mostly are derived from the lower body. Given that fact, the first essential mechanic to be discussed is one that virtually every top-flight quarterback in the world does on virtually every single throw. He has a wide base. The necessity to have a wide base is based on many reasons. Not only does this regimen apply to football, it also pertains to every other sport.

If you watch other positions in football, for example, linebackers, when they get in a stance, what do their feet look like? Are they close together or are they spread out with a nice wide base? When an offensive lineman gets in a stance, is his stance narrow, with his feet close together, or does he have a wide base? What about in basketball, when an individual is really dug in to play great defense, his feet are wide, and he is ready to go. Whether it's a golfer on the first tee, about to hit a big drive, a tennis player on the baseline, about to return a serve, or a boxer, about to deliver a knockout blow, all of these athletes have a wide base.

If your feet are close together, you have no balance. If your feet are close together, you can't generate power. If your feet are close together you don't have room to shift your weight.

It is impossible to generate as much power as possible when the quarterback's feet are close together. As such, one of the goals of every quarterback and every quarterback coach should be to do whatever is necessary to enable the quarterback to throw with more power. A wide base allows him to do that. A wide base allows him to drive off that back leg.

Even more importantly is the fact that a wide base doesn't allow the quarterback to commit the cardinal sin of overstriding. If a quarterback overstrides, it is impossible for him to have maximum weight shift, because his weight can never get back all the way through. If the weight shift doesn't get all the way through, then it is impossible to generate maximum power.

If the quarterback doesn't have a wide base, and he overstrides, his arm is always behind his body during his release and can never catch up. If the quarterback's arm is behind his body, he is losing accuracy. His ball will tend to sail or go in the dirt. Having his base shoulder-width apart or slightly wider will ensure that his arm is always in sync with his body.

What is a wide base? I teach my quarterbacks to get their feet shoulder-width apart or slightly wider than shoulder-width apart.

The ability to move in either direction, if the quarterback is flushed from the pocket or has to move within the pocket, is crucial to every quarterback. On occasion, a quarterback will have his feet so close together that he has to step first, get to his base, and then take off or move. When he does that, he is losing valuable time. Even though it's less than a second, it still slows down the quarterback's escape and reduces his ability to move with precision. Every position, especially the quarterback position, being in a balanced or "football position" is essential on every play.

Every drill I recommend relates to some sort of pass the quarterback must hit with a base. If you watch the greatest quarterbacks in the game today, you will see the vast majority of them play with a base and throw with a base almost every time. When they move in the pocket, they get into their base. If they are being harassed and have to get rid of the ball, they try to get their feet right.

Figure 4-1. The wide base of a quarterback

When they drop back, whether it's a three-step, five-step, or seven-step drop, they will hit with piston-like precision every time, because their movements are ingrained into their routine, which is their comfort zone. Comparatively speaking, this movement sequence is their free-throw scenario, in which they dribble the ball three times, and then drain the shot. Getting into the proper position to throw the ball is what the most consistent quarterbacks in the game do. They play with a great base, and they do it every possible time. The key point to remember is that this attribute has a positive impact on their level of power and accuracy, as well as their ability to shift their weight, which will lead to more consistency. Everything starts with having a wide base.

❏ Weight back. The next factor that needs to occur after the quarterback gets his feet slightly wider than his shoulders is getting his weight back. One observation that can reinforce the importance of having the weight back is to consider the great home run hitters in the game of baseball when they come to the plate. Have you ever watched them in their stance? Have you ever seen a great home run hitter stand in the box straight up and down, with no weight back?

In reality, they have so much weight on their back foot that their front foot often comes completely off the ground. Why do you think that is? It entails a weight shift. It involves transferring power. It is called having your weight back, driving off that back leg, getting your hips through for maximum power, and then shifting your weight.

If your quarterback is standing straight up and down and his weight is evenly distributed, there is no way he is achieving maximum power in his throws. What about the heavyweight boxer? If he is trying to knock someone out, he has his weight back. What about the tennis player who is serving for match point? His weight has also shifted back. In order to get everything he's got into his serve, he throws the ball high in the air and leans back, which is shifting his weight.

When a quarterback says he has his weight back, what does that mean? How much weight back should he have? While the numbers are a little arbitrary, I tell my quarterbacks to have a 75 percent to 25 percent distribution, i.e., 75 percent of his weight should shift back. When I first started coaching quarterbacks, I believed in an 80/20 weight shift. Over the years, I've come to feel that a 75/25 distribution is more realistic. Certainly, a 75/25 distribution puts the quarterback in a little better football position when it's time for him to deliver the ball.

As noted previously, the weight-back factor certainly applies to other sports. For example, if you attend any baseball game and watch the pitcher, you will see him shift 100 percent of his weight, when he is on the rubber, if he is winding up. If he is pitching from the stretch that is somewhat more like a quarterback standing in the pocket, throwing the football. If you watch the pitcher pitching from the stretch, you will see his weight go back, as he drives off his back leg and off the mound. If you have a quarterback who is standing relatively upright when he passes the ball, he doesn't have his weight back. As a result, he is losing big-time power on almost all of his throws.

Figure 4-2. The quarterback should have his weight on his back foot.

Having his weight back can ensure that the quarterback will be able to deliver a ball with the maximum amount of power possible. As a consequence, he will have more juice on his throws on in-cuts and curl routes. In turn, he will also have more velocity on out-cuts to the field and boundary. Having his weight back will result in adding several more yards on his throws on takeoff or go routes. What quarterback doesn't want more juice on his throws?

❏ A short step with his lead foot. While the first two components of great footwork technique are vital for the championship quarterback, the third element is also critical. In order to ensure that he has the utmost accuracy, the quarterback has to take a short step with his lead foot during the delivery. Usually, this step is about four to six inches. Over the years, I've gone away from talking about the four to six inches as much, because, sometimes, a taller quarterback with longer legs might step a little farther with his lead foot. As a result, his short step might not be quite as short as that of an under-six-foot quarterback.

What I do coach my quarterbacks on every day is to have a wide base and their weight back in order to ensure that they don't overstride. When quarterbacks overstride, it kills their capacity to be a consistent passer. Can a quarterback complete passes if he overstrides? Of course he can. It does, however, have a negative impact on his consistency.

A common assessment technique can be employed to determine if he is stepping properly when he passes the ball. You should be able to take a rod and drive it straight down from the palm of the quarterback's hand, through the tip of his chest, right through his kneecap, and down through the ball of his foot on his lead leg when he's releasing the football.

Figure 4-3. The quarterback should take a short step with his lead foot during delivery.

Figure 4-4. The proper release point for a quarterback

Previously, it was noted that the reason it is so crucial for a quarterback to have that wide base is because it prevents him from overstriding. Unfortunately, overstriders are everywhere. It doesn't matter if it's a youth camp, a junior high quarterback, or a highly recruited high school player, they are everywhere and everybody has them.

You can watch any college game on Saturdays, and if you really watch closely, you will see quarterbacks with very inconsistent footwork. These players constantly overstride, which causes them major accuracy problems.

It is so bad with some quarterbacks that you can actually hear their feet and heels click when they finish their drop and lose their base. I refer to them as "heel clickers." Heel clickers typically click their heels, and then promptly take about a three-foot stride, which causes the ball to go anywhere and everywhere. Typically, the heel clickers take a long stride. As a result, the ball will usually sail or go into the dirt. Their arm can't come close to catching up with the rest of their body, which makes it anatomically impossible to have consistent accuracy.

Every throwing drill I have my quarterbacks do is done with the quarterback having to end up at the top of his drop, with a wide base and his weight back. This technique has to be automatic every single time, if you want your quarterback to be a consistent passer who will lead his team to the championship. I don't have any quarterbacks do a bunch of pretty-looking drills. Instead, I make them game-related, i.e., they address fundamental mechanics in a way that enhances their ability to consistently throw completions. I want to make sure that what I refer to as the moment of truth, i.e., the time that the quarterback hits with his base until he releases the ball, the quarterback has given himself the best chance to throw an accurate pass. I coach this factor on every play of every practice.

❏ Step slightly to the left of the target. Another factor that is essential to champion-level quarterback play is the ability to shift all of his weight through whenever he steps with his lead foot. Inexplicably, some coaches continue to advocate having the quarterback step to his target. That advice is just false, in my opinion. In reality, the importance of having the quarterback step slightly to the left of his target if he is right-handed cannot be overstated.

A hypothetical example can help clarify the situation. If you step with your lead foot directly at your target, try putting both of your hands on your hips, with your fingers pointed out. Subsequently, you will see that your hips are at about 2 o'clock. If your hips are pointed at 2 o'clock, then your hips aren't as open as they need to be to get all your weight shifted. To a certain degree, it can also be seen that you are throwing against your body.

As was pointed out previously, I love to watch pitchers pitch. About 10 years ago, I watched a famous pitcher of a major league baseball team, who was young and about to become unfathomably rich. Watching him warm up, I kept seeing his lead foot be so closed to his target that he was actually stepping at about 3 o'clock. I kept watching in amazement—inning after inning. I kept thinking to myself that if he is stepping like this, how many miles per hour is he losing on his fastball because of not getting all of his weight shifted?

Mechanically, he wasn't perfect, but he was talented, and he could really bring the heat. What happened next made me really stop and think that these mechanics not only help you throw with more power and accuracy, but they also help keep your arm healthy. About two months later, this young stud pitcher developed arm problems, and although he came back, he was never able to regain the magic that he had created. Subsequently, he ended up having to retire early the next season.

This scenario with this young pitcher opened up a whole new world for me. Not only were the mechanics we advocated helping our quarterbacks fundamentally, they were helping them not have to deal with sore arms and elbows. Our quarterbacks throw as much as anywhere I've ever been. Not once has a quarterback been lost to a sore arm. Our quarterbacks do not miss reps or practices, because what they are taught is anatomically correct.

Figure 4-5. The quarterback stepping at the target; notice his closed hips

Ideally, the quarterback should step about two inches to the left of his target, if he is right-handed. This positioning will allow him to get maximum weight shift. The following exercise can help him see whether he is stepping properly. If he puts his hands on his hips, with his fingers pointed out and then steps slightly to the left of an imaginable target, he can see that his hips are directly in line with his target. In turn, if his hips are directly in line with his target, he can then get 100 percent of his weight shifted.

Figure 4-6. The quarterback stepping to the left of
the target; notice the quarterback's hips to the target

To this point in the chapter, the discussion has focused on proper throwing mechanics, all of which have been lower-body related. The importance of a quarterback having a wide base, with his weight back, has been pointed out, as has the absolute necessity of the quarterback not to take a long lead step and overstride. All-in-all, the factors that have been examined so far are of paramount importance to the ability of a quarterback to throw with maximum velocity, accuracy, and consistency.

❏ The elbow parallel to the ground or higher. The next factor that is critical for a quarterback being able to be an accurate passer is the first upper body mechanic—the quarterback's release point. His release point should encompass a point where his elbow is parallel to the ground or higher. There have been very few quarterbacks of an elite status who have thrown with a low elbow or thrown with a sidearm motion. Quarterbacks who have a low release generally miss more throws and lack consistency as passers.

Low-elbow quarterbacks are kind of like the person who throws darts in a pub. Those individuals are aimers. They drop their elbow and then aim. When quarterbacks start dropping their elbow and aiming, a less-accurate pass is almost guaranteed.

Figure 4-7. The low-release point of the quarterback

A quarterback wants to stay on top and drive the ball toward his target. Low-elbow quarterbacks can't do that. Low-elbow quarterbacks can't throw a swing route over a defender, without the ball taking off and sailing. Low-elbow quarterbacks will get many more of their passes batted down by defenders, because of the release point. A quarterback with a low elbow cannot throw a ball over a defender, without the nose of the ball being up, which can cause it to take off and sail like a punt on occasion.

Drills that can help low-delivery quarterbacks will be detailed later in this book. These drills are not an overnight remedy. In fact, they have to be done on a regular basis for months. Furthermore, the quarterback has to be willing to work relentlessly on his delivery. He also has to sincerely want to change his delivery, or it will not happen.

Personally, I won't even recruit a quarterback who has a low-elbow or sidearm release, because it takes too much time to correct it. All factors considered, I'd rather just go ahead and recruit a quarterback who has a nice high release and help him improve on that, as well as in other areas of his game. As a rule, a low-elbow quarterback is an athlete who is going to be big-time high maintenance. Furthermore, he can revert back to his old habits during the most stressful of times. When that occurs, he will be throwing incompletions. Not only will he not be consistent enough to win games, he will not lead his team to championships.

Figure 4-8. The quarterback's elbow should be
parallel to the ground or higher on his release point.

❏ A "Z" in the knee. The next factor that is required for championship-level quarterback play is for the quarterback to land with flexion in his lead leg, a technique that sometimes is referred to as landing with a "Z" in the knee. Too many times, quarterbacks land with a locked lead leg. Sometimes, it is so violent that the quarterback looks like he is going to hyperextend his knee. When a quarterback doesn't land with a slight bend in his knee, it causes all of the momentum of the weight shift to come to a complete halt.

The scenario is similar to a golfer who short-arms his nine iron on his approach to the green and his follow-through stops. It could also be compared to a baseball player who after he hits the ball, his bat comes to a stop. When a situation much the same on a gridiron occurs, the quarterback will lose his weight shift, which, in turn, makes him lose valuable momentum and power on his finish. The ability to have a bend in the lead leg enables a quarterback to get five to eight more yards on a deep ball. It also allows the quarterback to have maximum zip on the ball. Any time the leg is locked, the quarterback will lose the final aspect of a complete weight shift.

Figure 4-9. The quarterback with a "Z" in his knee

❏ The head still. Another essential factor with regard to power, accuracy, and consistently being able to complete passes is an element that is very rarely talked about, but is very important when it comes to accuracy—the quarterback must keep his head still. Quarterbacks who try to throw the ball extremely hard and try to get as much juice as possible on a throw sometimes end up jerking their head off of their target. The quarterback must keep his head still. If he doesn't keep his head still, as he is explosively coming through on his release, he can end up pulling the ball to his left if you are a right-handed quarterback.

I once had a quarterback who was small, but played big. While he had a pretty decent arm for such a little individual, I kept noticing that he was missing throws to his left. I checked and rechecked every snap of practice and still I couldn't figure it out. All of the previously discussed, essential mechanics for a quarterback seemed to be checking out.

Finally, after a lot of reps and after I studied him carefully, I figured out that he was trying to get so much juice on his ball and was doing everything in his power to get as much velocity on the ball as possible, his head was coming with his off-arm as he threw. Because he was jerking his head to the left, he was pulling his ball to the left as well. Once the cause of his problem was determined, it was easy to point out to him and show him on tape what he was doing. As a result, we were able to get it corrected easily. Once his head became still again, he went back to putting the ball where he wanted and became the accurate passer that he had always been.

❑ The follow-through. The final mechanical aspect of a championship quarterback's release is his follow-through. This last phase of the release should consist of the lead leg having a slight bend in it, i.e., a "Z" in it. His back leg should come off the ground, much like a pitcher's leg does when coming off the mound. I've heard big-time quarterback coaches claim that the back leg should just drag on the ground. How many pitchers have you seen who just have their back leg scrape the ground? None, I can tell you. If a quarterback's release isn't violent enough to make his back leg come off the ground, or if he is purposefully not bringing his back leg all the way through and off the ground, I can guarantee that the quarterback isn't throwing with as much power as he is capable of.

What should the quarterback's throwing arm look like on a great follow-through? It should come down and finish low around his left thigh pad on a right-handed quarterback. I was once around a quarterback who had such a strong arm and such great arm whip that his hand would actually bounce off his thigh pad. By any reasonable measure, the ball was really coming out of there. It came out with such force that a bystander could actually hear it whistle though the air. Believe it or not, his ball was so loud that his offensive linemen could hear the ball while they were in the act of pass protecting.

By design, to this point, the chapter has focused very little on the upper body. As discussed previously, the majority of a quarterback's power, accuracy, and consistency come from his lower body. The only factor related to the upper body so far is for the quarterback to have the elbow on his throwing arm parallel to the ground or higher. There are, however, a couple of upper-body mechanics that are crucial to the art of throwing a football.

❑ The lead shoulder pointed to the target. The first factor entails the quarterback putting his lead shoulder on his target. There are two main reasons this should be done. One, it generates more power because if his lead shoulder is not facing the target, he isn't getting his torso fully rotated, which means he is losing power. Second, if he keeps his lead shoulder on his target, he has a consistent target for which to aim. If his shoulder never gets far enough over to his target, he will have an inconsistent target because his shoulder will be open at arbitrary angles. As a result, he will have a potentially different release point with every pass.

It is not uncommon to see quarterbacks warming up, who never put their lead shoulder on their target. They should be made to get it right. The goal is to milk out the last bit of power through great mechanics. This factor is one of them. Just like in boxing, a jab is much less powerful than a right-hand cross. Why? No hip rotation occurs with a jab. When a fighter throws his right cross, he is getting full shoulder rotation, and his hips are coming through to the target. Yes, even boxers have to have great weight shift to deliver a knockout blow. Requiring a quarterback to have his shoulder to his target is a relatively easy thing to coach. Focusing on this mechanic should start early every day, when the quarterback is warming up before practice.

Finally, if everything occurs as intended, the quarterback has gotten to the top of his drop and has his weight back, with his feet in a wide base. He has stepped slightly to the left of his target, and he has his throwing elbow parallel to the ground or higher. He has a "Z" in his knee. It's now time to let the ball go.

❑ The elbow drives down by the rib cage. When he releases the football, his left arm should be bent at 90 degrees. That bent elbow should drive down violently, close to his rib cage. After he's driven his left elbow, his back foot should come off the ground to finish the throw. If he has an inconsistent left elbow, and if it's not driving down, almost skimming the rib cage, causing the elbow to start to fly out, the result can be that the quarterback pulls the ball, as well. His left elbow has to be constant, just like his head has to be still, in order not to pull the ball off line.

A List of the Common Mechanics of a Powerful, Accurate, and Consistent Passer

- A wide base
- Weight back
- A short step with his lead foot
- Step slightly to the left of the target
- The elbow parallel to the ground or higher
- A "Z" in the knee
- The head still
- The follow-through
- The lead shoulder pointed to the target
- The elbow drives down by the rib cage

The Chapter in Review

A number of ways exist to coach a quarterback the mechanics of throwing, just like there are many ways to teach a golfer the proper way to swing a golf club. I know that when I had a couple of golf lessons, I had so many things going through my head even before I swung the club, it was almost impossible for me to concentrate on the basics of just hitting the ball.

In reality, a similar scenario applies to a quarterback. This chapter detailed 10 different factors that are crucial in developing consistent power and accuracy in a quarterback. Undoubtedly, there are lots of quarterback coaches in the game, who have had great success, who have an extensive and different checklist of how to throw the football effectively.

Personally, however, I believe that the best way to teach and coach the mechanics of throwing is to simplify them as much as you can. Get down to just a few essential elements. As a result, the quarterback won't get bogged down by trying to do all 100 things. When that occurs, you've got a quarterback who is thinking way too much on something that can be really simple, if it's presented really simply. I coach every kid on every throw of every day. If you present the essential information in an easy-to-understand, straightforward manner, your quarterback will know it like you do, and he will be able to self-correct off the tape, before you ever say a word to him.

CHAPTER 5
Daily Checklist

In my opinion, consistency starts with routines. I believe that teams and individuals want order and consistency when they pertain to the game of football. This factor is no different for great quarterbacks. Quarterbacks want structure and consistent routines. Given that, over the years, I developed several key daily practice components for a quarterback. If those aspects are presented and worked on every single day in practice, a quarterback will be well on his way into developing into a championship quarterback.

Some of the factors are related to the mentality of the quarterback. Others are things that we physically practice every day, including the following:

- Don't take sacks.
- Never say "don't throw an interception" to the quarterback.
- Scramble to throw.
- Throw against the blitz every day.
- Know whom to throw to on the blitz.
- Protect the quarterback inside-out.
- Have the quarterback deceive with his eyes and his actions.
- Require the quarterback to help coach the wide receivers.
- Put the quarterback in adverse situations in practice.
- Force the quarterback to make difficult throws in practice.

- Don't take sacks. It could be argued that times exist when taking a sack is OK. For example, if the house is caving in on him, and the quarterback has no recourse but to take the sack, then that is something that obviously has to be done. With every pass play that we teach, aside from the obvious outlet or check-down, we talk about how and when the quarterback can throw the ball away to avoid taking the sack. He knows on every pass play that is installed where his closest receiver will be, and if he's in trouble, he should just get the ball close to a receiver, so that he doesn't have to take the sack.

  Sacks are not a good thing. Sacks are momentum-killers. Sacks destroy drives. Sacks are hidden yardage lost. Sacks affect field position, because they are so hard to overcome.

  Since the beginning of time, field position has been crucial in the game of football. A number of studies have been done concerning the percentages of scoring a touchdown, based on how close a team is to the goal line. Sacks take you farther away from the first-down chains, as well as further away from the end zone. As such, sacks must be avoided at all costs.

  The red zone sack could be the worst of all sacks. Taking sacks in the red zone is a cardinal sin. Anything that compromises points is a very bad thing. A sack in the red zone not only hurts your chances of scoring a touchdown, it also hurts the chances of you being able to kick a field goal. While it may be obvious, sacks in the red zone will get good teams beat.

  We practice weekly throwing the ball away in the red zone. I will take the quarterback down close to the end zone and have him physically practice throwing the ball away, i.e., have someone, even myself sometimes, simulate a pass rush and also have someone stand where the quarterback's check-down will be and have him practice throwing the ball away. This exercise is a great drill, because the quarterback should know that when you get to the red zone, the game speeds up. The closer you get to the goal line, the faster the game becomes. He knows before every pass play called that he has to get rid of the football and not take a sack.

  Every time one of my quarterbacks goes down to the end zone area to practice in the red zone, I am in his ear saying, "No sacks; take care of the ball." If the quarterback takes a sack in the red zone, he is going to get lit up by me. Our goal is to never take a sack, ever.

- Never say "don't throw an interception" to the quarterback. You will never hear me say something like that to the quarterback. Those negative words and thoughts will never come out of my mouth, and they shouldn't come out of yours. A very fine line exists for a quarterback in trying to make a play and forcing the football into places it shouldn't go. Your job as a coach is to know his physical abilities and to help him understand what throws he can make and what throws he can't.

  I never want to put a negative thought in the quarterback's head, because I don't want him to be afraid to try and make a play. You want your quarterback to be confident in his arm and confident in his ability to make a throw in a crucial situation. If your quarterback is afraid to make a play and plays cautiously, it will inhibit your offense and take away some of your big-play capabilities.

Instead of telling the quarterback not to throw an interception, I tell him to take care of the football. That point also applies to the running backs. I always tell the running backs to carry the ball high and tight, as opposed to telling them, don't fumble the football. Furthermore, it goes for offensive linemen too. Instead of saying, don't jump off sides or don't hold, I say, listen to the snap count and be locked in to it. Instead of telling them not to hold, I tell them to keep their hands inside.

Do you really want your wide receiver thinking don't drop this ball, or do you want him thinking to watch the ball all the way into his hands? The same factor applies with your quarterback. You should paint positive pictures for him, not negative ones.

For a quarterback, there is a big difference in trying to make a play and forcing a football into a route that is well-covered. Similarly, there is a big difference in trying to make a play and throwing the ball up for grabs in a crowd. Quarterbacks who force balls will get you beat. When and if they do try to force their throws, I am going to light them up.

We always try to put positive thoughts into our players' heads. On the other hand, if your quarterback tries to force balls into places he shouldn't, it will be hard to justify playing him. You want your quarterback to be confident in his abilities to make a throw, but also smart enough to know when to simply throw the ball away.

❏ Scramble to throw. Some of the biggest plays in football are a result of a quarterback who moves out of the pocket and finds a receiver 30 or 40 yards down the field, for example, and throws it to him for a big completion. It can be argued that these plays are like free-yardage plays. They are similar to a punt return, in that there is a lot of space to cover, if you are a defender. As a result, the defender better stay disciplined in his coverage responsibilities, or a big play could take place.

The key in scrambling to throw is the quarterback's eyes must be downfield. Some quarterbacks just take off and run. On occasion, that's great. The bigger plays, however, are the ones in which he spots an open receiver way down the field and gets him the ball.

In my opinion, you can teach a quarterback to scramble to throw even if it's not his natural instinct. There are a couple of steps that I take to help ensure that he is capable of executing effectively in a scramble situation. The first thing that we do in our individual drills is to set up a scramble situation, in which I stand where I can see his eyes. After he gets flushed from the pocket, as he is moving, I will watch him like a hawk to make sure that his eyes are downfield, trying to find a receiver. You don't even have to throw a ball in this drill. All you want to have happen is, after he moves, make sure that his eyes are downfield. This drill can enhance his eye discipline if it is performed frequently enough.

The second technique that we employ to help develop the ability of our quarterbacks to scramble is every day during one or more of our pass skeleton drills, we whisper "scramble" to the quarterback. We don't tell anyone else. No one on defense and no one on offense will know, only the quarterback. This exercise is a great drill because everyone benefits. It is great for the defense because they have scramble rules, just like the offense does. Not only does it help with the defense's discipline downfield, it also helps the wide receivers, tight ends, and running backs apply their scramble rules, as well.

When you whisper to your quarterback to scramble, it is important that you are standing where you can see his eyes. It is also critical that he not be allowed to just scramble one way and then throw. Make him scramble to his right, hold the ball, and then move back to his left. Such a requirement doesn't have to be in effect all of the time. It's great, however, because it makes the defense stay disciplined longer than they are used to. It also improves the likelihood that your scramble rules are fully understood by all of your offensive players and how they are applied when the ball is moving away from them.

Obviously, the procedure is great for the quarterback, because he can better gain a feel of what throws he is capable of making under duress. It also teaches him that about nine times out of 10, if he is scrambling to throw, he can't throw back behind him, because those balls are getting ready to be intercepted. I've been fortunate to have several quarterbacks over the years who, when they left the pocket, I got excited because I knew something big was about to happen. In scramble situations, if you have done a good job as a coach, you won't be anxious when he leaves the pocket because you know something good is about to happen or, at worst, nothing bad will occur, because of the training the quarterback received from you.

❏ Throw against the blitz every day. Because of the nature of the defenses utilized by teams in recent years, it is imperative to throw against the blitz on a daily basis. Back when I first started coaching, there weren't many teams that would blitz with as high a percentage as teams do in the game today. In fact, a number of bring some sort of pressure over 50 percent of the time on every down. Back in the day, the only blitz you saw might be on third down, and it was going to be a pressure, with man-to-man coverage.

At the present time, there are a lot of defensive coordinators who like to come on first down to set you behind the sticks, i.e., put you in long-yardage situations on second and third down. Second down becomes that same mentality with some teams. If you have a second-and-five situation, for example, defenses will blitz to make you have to execute a relatively long third-down conversion.

In football today, third down has become a science project. You will encounter different fronts and coverages. You will face odd fronts, even though they may like to be a four-defender-down team. You will see both zone pressures and man pressures. Not only does your quarterback have to know how to handle consistent pressure, your offensive line and running backs also have to know how to apply all of their protection rules within the context of all of the pressures they are going to see that week.

It is important that your offense, especially your quarterback, is comfortable in handling all the different pressures. I always tell our entire offense (including the quarterback), I hope they blitz. I hope they come after us.

With all the pressures that you may face, you have to practice the pressures, and you have to be confident in how to block them and pick them up. Your quarterback has to know what to do with the ball every time. He has to know the different front and blitz looks and which of those looks mandates a change in his protection. He has to be comfortable with communicating with his teammates, because there will be times when a lot of communication is needed.

If you practice against pressure enough, you should be able to have a very confident quarterback, as well as a very confident offense. If you tell your team that if the defense comes after them, they are going to pay, you can generally get offenses excited. In fact, more often than not, you may actually get your offense hoping they do get blitzed, because they know they are ready to hit some big plays. In reality, if your quarterback has seen enough film and has practiced against the blitz enough, in most instances, he will be able to tell, pre-snap, what the defense is about to do.

One of the first things we do when we start practice for the upcoming game is to introduce all of the different blitzes of that opponent that we have seen on tape. We then carry that over every day on the practice field until game time. Your quarterback should end up seeing pressure every day at practice. Even in the walk-through on the day of the game, there should be some sort of blitz review. He should be dialed in and ready to attack the opponent's pressures with his own answers. I always tell our players that if the defense is a pressure team, it has nothing else to go to if their pressures aren't working. What are they going to do, go back and play base defense? If they do that, we really are in position to have the upper hand.

❏ Know whom to throw to on the blitz. Every pass in your arsenal has to have blitz answers. Every throw against pressure must be executed by your entire offense, especially your quarterback. He has to know who to throw to in every blitz situation. It may be a "hot" receiver, i.e., a predetermined route by a predetermined receiver in response to a certain pressure. In those instances, he has to know who is hot on every blitz. If he doesn't have a hot receiver on a particular pressure, the quarterback must know what route is being used against the pressure. He has to know what his answer is on every play against every pressure.

The film room is a great place to start with ingraining in the quarterback to whom he should throw on a blitz. There aren't many teams out there that disguise their pressures well enough all of the time for the quarterback not to have a significant idea that something is coming. Once you have imprinted all of the blitz looks in his head through watching film, it's then time to go outside and walk through what he just watched. After that, it's time to practice full speed versus all the pressures. It is hard to simulate with a scout team all of the different alignments, especially in the secondary all of the time.

The aforementioned is why your film study and walk-through is so important. Your quarterback should know the alignments of the defenders on each blitz to the point that he can align the defenders himself during practice. If you are playing a team that likes to come after you, your quarterback has to know when and where to change his protection. He also better know whom to throw the ball to on every single play on which he is getting pressured. If your quarterback has been trained properly, and he knows what he is getting ready to do before the play even begins, you have a quarterback who is going to be highly successful.

❑ Protect the quarterback inside-out. In other words, he is going to be secured from B gap to B gap. There is nothing worse to me than giving up an A or B gap run-through. Those defenders have the straightest shot to the quarterback. They can hurt your quarterback quicker than a rusher coming from the outside, because he gets there faster. In those instances, if the quarterback isn't getting hit hard, he is having to throw over some of those bodies quicker than he may want to. Not only are the defenders taking the shortest route to the quarterback, the receiver's routes haven't had time to develop.

If all of the pressures are forced to come from the outside, at least the quarterback has time to adjust and just throw the ball away, if the situation so dictates. Not only can he see a pressure easier from an outside defender, he also has more time to decide what to do with the ball. If you give up an A gap or B gap run-through, it destroys the timing of the receiver's routes worse than a defender coming from the outside. When that occurs, obviously, the offense's chances for success on the play have diminished drastically.

When the fact that your quarterback can get hurt faster from an inside run-through is combined with the point that an inside rusher destroys the timing of your pass play faster than an outside rusher can, it's easy to see why you should devise your protections in a way to handle pressure from the inside-out. Even in these days of getting five receivers out and, in some cases, lining up without a back in the backfield, your mindset should be to protect your quarterback from the inside-out.

❑ Have the quarterback deceive with his eyes and his actions. One of the most overlooked aspects of effective quarterback play is the art of deception with a quarterback's eyes and actions. This attribute is a lost art in today's quarterback play. The point that needs to be emphasized is not that people don't teach it much anymore, it's just real hard to see any quarterbacks who adhere to this precept who aren't playing in the National Football League.

Defensive backs and linebackers are taught to read the quarterback's eyes. They can get a jump before the ball is even out of the quarterback's hands, if they study their opponent and the quarterback in their upcoming contest. Accordingly, it is much easier if the quarterback learns to move defenders with his eyes.

There are times when looking a defender off doesn't apply. For example, if the quarterback is on a three-step drop, and the ball is coming out right now, it's not necessary to try and move a defender. However, if a route is called that has two receivers going up both hash marks, and the defense has only one centerfield free safety, the quarterback most definitely needs to steer him one way with his eyes, knowing that he wants to throw to the other receiver.

Another example of a quarterback moving a defender with his eyes and actions involves moving a linebacker one way or another, because the play entails underneath crossing routes coming or a shallow cross and a dig coming behind it.

Another scenario in which it is beneficial for the quarterback to move defenders with his eyes is on screen passes. For example, some sort of double screen is called and the quarterback knows which side he is working, because of what the defense has presented prior to the snap. He can look one way, maybe even give a pump-fake, and then turn and throw the ball in the direction he knew he wanted to work the whole time anyway.

There are a number of ways to get defenders to lean. Some coaches, for example, teach their players to drive on the ball the instant the quarterback takes his off hand off of the ball. That is generally a good time to drive on a ball, because, in most cases, when the off hand comes off of the ball, the quarterback has made his decision on where the ball is going, and he is getting ready to fire the ball.

As discussed previously, a quarterback does not need to look the defender off on every pass route. On the routes that involve a vertical stretch on a defender, who is hi-lowed, a good look-off or a slight pump-fake can make all of the difference between a completion and an incompletion. The same factor applies to horizontal stretches. On numerous occasions, a quarterback can move a defender by giving him some cheese in the direction the defender wants to go anyway. Another hypothetical situation could entail a simple curl route, with another receiver in the flat. If the flat defender is running hard to the flat, the quarterback can just lean in the direction of the receiver in the flat and reinforce the decision the defender has already made, knowing that the ball is going to the curl route.

When I teach pump-fakes, I don't teach keeping two hands on the ball like some coaches do. I understand that you don't want the ball to slip out of the quarterback's hand on the pump-fake but I also know that those coaches on the other side of the argument teach that once the off hand comes off, drive on the ball. Quarterback coaches need to understand and have a feeling for what routes could use a little deception with the quarterback's eyes and actions, and then make it a priority to coach. If the importance of a particular point is stressed frequently enough to the quarterback, he will work at it. Ultimately, it will be very nice for everyone to get some easy completions, because the quarterback has fooled a defender with his eyes or his actions.

❑ Require the quarterback to help coach the wide receivers. This factor doesn't always go over all that well with the wide receiver coach. On the other hand, in my opinion, it's essential to the level of communication between the two, as well as the quarterback's feel of the passing game, in general, when these two are constantly talking and interacting.

The value of such communication can be substantial. For example, a receiver is supposed to run a 15-yard dig, but came out of his break early. The quarterback needs to tell him he was short on his route. It doesn't matter what the situation is, the quarterback needs to coach his receivers, because they are the athletes playing the game. I don't care how good of a coach you are, or how great a feel you might have for a particular team or a specific game, your feel isn't as good as the individuals who are out there playing.

The aforementioned is why I talk to the quarterbacks in the first quarterback meeting of the year to make sure that they will be coaching the wideouts. In reality, a number of instances exist, in which I am up in the box, and I may be looking at the point of attack, while the receiver coach is signaling and trying to watch three other wideouts on a play. Subsequently, we both miss something that we should have or could have seen. The point to be emphasized is that it is essential that you require your quarterback to coach the receivers. Nothing should be permitted to get past us on game day.

As long as the quarterback is communicating in a respectful manner, I've never seen a receiver get mad or resent the quarterback for coaching and communicating with him. I've always felt that the receiver wants the ball to be thrown to him as often as possible. Furthermore, he wants the quarterback to say something to him if anything occurs that might otherwise interfere with him getting the ball.

The only negative circumstance that occasionally transpires when the quarterback is coaching the wide receivers is a situation in which the quarterback makes excuses, when it's his fault. Coaches need to be alert for this factor to see if it unfolds at practice. I've seen some finger-pointers at the quarterback spot. If he doesn't own up to his mistakes, e.g., his missed reads and throws, then a problem could occur. In all honesty, if that is happening, you are playing the wrong kid at quarterback.

Great leaders take responsibility for their mistakes. Furthermore, when the circumstances of the situation are in doubt, they will often take the blame off of their teammates. The point to remember is that if you have a quarterback who is trying to pass the buck then you are not playing the right guy.

A number of examples exist concerning what your quarterback could coach the receiver on in practice or a game. It could be route depths. It could be that he stopped pumping his arms in his route, indicating that he is getting ready to break off his route, when he wasn't. It could be a missed hot. It could be making the receiver aware of how critical his block is on this particular play.

Most of the receivers that I've been around in my coaching career love communicating with their quarterback. It makes them feel more in tune with what's going on. It also makes them want to play hard and play well for their on-the-field general.

❏ Put the quarterback in adverse situations in practice. This aspect is right at the top of the developmental process for a championship quarterback. What does this factor entail? It means you aren't cheating for him during the blitz pick-up drill. He is required to see the blitz on his own. If he doesn't see it, he has to reap the consequences. It means having him execute a pitch on an option play against which you might have incorporated the toughest look possible, a defensive response that happens faster in the practice exercise than it will during the game. It means giving him some looks that he hasn't seen or discussed to determine if he can and will apply his rules to help him have success.

Having the quarterback deal with adversity also entails not telling him what defensive looks he is about to see before the ball is snapped. Unfortunately, a number of coaches coach this way (i.e., feed the quarterback the look pre-snap) just to cover their own butt. That approach is not going to win you a ballgame on game day, when you are essentially cheating the drill to make yourself or your player look good during practice. It gives everyone a false sense of security, which is not good when you go try and win a ballgame.

Another set of circumstances in which you can put your quarterback in adverse situations occurs during spring ball against your defense. In this situation, you don't call plays or put in special plays that you know will work, because the quarterback sees this particular defense every day. Instead, you force him to execute against stacked lines of your own defense and force him to go through his progressions against a coverage look that is very tough to defeat on a particular route.

I've been around a number of defensive coaches who either tell their athletes what play is about to be run or tell their unit what a particular code word means. As such, they try to make their players look good during spring ball or fall camp. In my opinion, however, that mindset doesn't help anybody in the long run. Personally, I don't mind having your quarterback or your offensive unit sled uphill, so to speak, during drills and in team time, because in the long run, I feel like if you can execute your assignments against the toughest looks possible, it makes you better over time. In every drill, I not only do try to make it faster than it will be in a game, I also always try and give the quarterback the toughest looks possible.

The key point to remember is that if you put your quarterback in adverse situations in practice, it will make the game easier for him. If you are a coach who feels like he has to cover his own butt with the head coach, you aren't going to put your quarterback in the hot seat often enough to make his long term growth as good as it could/should be. As such, things will be too easy for him in practice. If you want a championship quarterback on game day, you have to put him in the situations that challenge him as much as possible during the week.

❏ Force the quarterback to make difficult throws in practice. If the quarterback doesn't practice making difficult throws in practice, how can he be expected to make difficult throws in the game?

Comparing the situation to another sport, do you think that basketball players just fire up turnaround jump shots or fade-away jumpers? Of course not. They spend hour upon hour practicing those difficult shots. The same scenario applies to a quarterback. How can you expect him to make hard throws, if you don't put him in a comparable situation in practice?

I try to put the quarterback in a variety of scenarios daily to have him ready to go, just in case he has to make a difficult throw in the game. For example, pretty much every day, I have the quarterback come out on a naked or bootleg fake and make him throw over a defender who is right in his face. The quarterback has to learn to raise his arm high and keep the same arm speed downward in his release.

During this drill, I make him throw over the outstretched hands of a defender. I also make him throw around the defender in a sidearm motion. In addition, I make him practice his pump-fake to get a defender in the air, so he can easily get around him, which makes his throw easier.

We practice these throws to the right and the left. We rapid fire these reps, so our quarterbacks can get multiple reps both ways each day. It never fails during the course of a season that this exact thing will happen with the quarterback booting out and have a big, tall defensive end in his face. Because of all of the reps the quarterback had practicing off-balance throws and tough throws, he is better prepared to make a tough situation easy, because he was ready for it.

Every day, we practice having the quarterback in the pocket. We then have a defensive player rush in with his hands up. In that situation, our quarterback practices raising his elbow while making a variety of different throws. On occasion, we work on having him throw a shallow cross with people in his face. We also vary the speed periodically with which the receiver comes running in order to make the quarterback work at not only getting the ball over the outstretched arms of a defender, but also having to judge how much to lead the receiver.

On occasion, we practice a throw to the back in the flat, simulating a hot situation, and require the quarterback to have to get the ball over the outstretched hands of the defender. Again, we try to simulate a defender who got a great jump on the snap count, which requires the quarterback to make his hot throw to his receiver, using a sidearm motion. We also practice fade balls, thrown deep into the end zone. In this exercise, I put my hat down, two yards from the back corner of the end zone. We then simulate the rush. The underlying objective is to have the quarterback make accurate throws under duress.

We typically have the quarterbacks compete to see who is going to make more throws during these drills. In the case of the fade route, whoever hits my hat the most often wins the competition. As before, we have our quarterbacks practice making the throws both to the right and the left.

Fortunately, every place I've worked, I haven't had to be involved in coaching special teams. Periods allotted to special teams are the best times to work on this kind of stuff, because we don't need any other players to help us. We can also get fast, concentrated work in, as well as have our own competition in all of these drills to spice practice up a little.

Generally, each week, we also work on a deep overcross from a receiver coming from the opposite side of the field. We set the drill up with the receiver running at full speed. Once the receiver sets his angle, I then have the quarterback drop back and have someone rush him. If there is no underneath coverage, and there is clearly an open area in which to drop the ball, the quarterback does that. If, on the other hand, a linebacker is sitting in coverage, the quarterback practices throwing the ball away. This exercise is a great drill, because it not only forces your quarterback to make the right decision on whether to throw the ball or not, it also requires him to work on throwing to an open area with finesse and precision.

In reality, you can develop your own drills that are appropriate for your team and your quarterback. Regardless of what specific drills you ultimately employ, it is absolutely essential that you require your quarterback to make difficult throws every day in practice, so that he can have an opportunity to be successful during the game.

CHAPTER 6
Pre-Snap Fundamentals

Championship quarterbacks are in complete control of a number of factors before the ball is even snapped. As such, in my opinion, a quarterback needs to do the exact same thing every time at the line of scrimmage. For example, his eyes need to do the exact same thing every time so that he does not tip off to the defense. Consequently, his routine becomes habit forming. In turn, he will acquire a certain degree of comfort that the great quarterbacks have that just adds to his confidence level.

One of the first factors that the quarterback must master is the play clock. As was discussed previously, no excuse exists for the quarterback to ever let the play clock run out, ever. In reality, I have gone entire years without a team having a delay of game penalty. To have such an infraction is poor coaching and even worse quarterback play. At all times, the quarterback has to know where his team is in relation to the play clock, and he has to play the game accordingly.

A number of factors are involved with being locked in to the 40-second clock. The first factor involved is what is the tempo you are trying to play? What is the situation? Are you trying to play fast, if you are an up-tempo team, or are you in a four-minute mode of operation? Obviously, if you are trying to go fast, you aren't worried about letting the clock wind down. If you are trying to milk the clock, because you are ahead, then you've got to understand that and not snap the ball with more than three seconds on the play clock.

Other factors are also involved with understanding all of the things that can come into play with the game clock. Down and distance is important. Your quarterback has to understand, before the snap, if his team is in a normal down-and-distance situation. Or, is his team facing a third-down and extra or a fourth-down situation?

Two additional considerations that are of major importance are whether the quarterback is facing a base defense or a nickel or dime defense. Where is the offense on the field? Is it backed up where it has to be extremely careful? Is it a goal-line or short-yardage situation? Is the offense contemplating a two-minute offense or a four-minute offense? Is the offense facing overtime, the possibility of a two-point play, or the last play of the half or game? How much time is left in the half or the game? What is the score?

The point to be emphasized is that every single one of these factors is critically important for a quarterback to know and understand before the ball is even snapped. A championship quarterback is the master of situational football. An integral part of why he has mastered the art of situational football is he understands the existing circumstance he is facing before the play or the drive ever begins.

One situation that has become almost lost in the modern day offenses of today is the team that huddles. In reality, a few teams exist that do huddle and use it to their advantage. One big advantage of huddling that has nothing to do with a team's style of play is the leadership qualities that come through to every member of the offense with a championship quarterback.

The quarterback with a fire in his eyes and a fire in his belly can almost will an offensive unit to succeed. Every great quarterback has great command in the huddle, an attribute that starts with all eyes on him. This air of distinction is not only expected, it's demanded by him. Once a team's field general steps in the huddle, all talking stops immediately.

While a number of different styles of huddles exist, all of them have one thing in common—every player can see the quarterback's mouth and eyes. Every great quarterback will communicate with his eyes, as well as with his aura of confidence. Every great quarterback has a way of letting a player with a big job on the play know it either through verbal or unspoken communication. For example, if it's a big ball going up, he will tell his offensive line to hold out the defense just a split second longer. If a wide receiver has to hold up a little longer on a perimeter run, he will let that particular player know it. In fact, every great quarterback that I've been around in my coaching career was great in the huddle. Every great quarterback will always give his team an extra "heads up," if it is a different snap count or a special alert or check. A great quarterback tends to have a feeling for whom he can get on to and whom he needs to motivate. As such, huddling offers tangible advantages for teams that huddle. Not surprisingly, every great quarterback that I've been around has been just super in the huddle.

For the teams that don't huddle, the quarterback has to be dynamic with his communication skills at the line of scrimmage. He has to hustle to the ball and be close to the ball, so that no time is lost. I always tell our quarterbacks that there can be no secrets on the field. For example, if any doubt exists concerning whether to communicate something or not, go ahead and make sure everyone is on the same page.

I have never worried too much about opponents getting my team's signals or teams honing in to my code words. If your team is good enough, there will be times when you've got to execute and win, when the other team knows exactly what you are running. At that moment of truth, you have to out-execute your opponent, as well as out-"want" them, if you are going to be a champion. True masters of the no-huddle offense are in complete control at all times. More often than not, they simply don't care whether their opponent knows exactly what is getting ready to happen on the next snap.

A number of different ways exist to line up and play defense. In general, defenses play either an odd (e.g., three-man) front or an even (four-man) front. Within that context, the quarterback should know going into the game what the base defense of his opponent is. The same factor applies to his opponent's base coverage.

After scanning the front left to right, I want our quarterbacks to scan through the linebackers to find the safeties. On numerous occasions, linebackers give away coverages and pressures more than any other position group on defense. As such, the quarterback needs to determine if the linebackers are playing in their normal location or are they cheating closer or leaning to a different gap? Is there a linebacker overload?

As the quarterback scans through the linebackers, are they playing with two safeties, or are they playing with one? If they look like they are playing with two, is there any tilt to their alignment, indicating a rotation of their coverage? What is the depth of both of their safeties? Is one safety at 10 yards and the other safety at 12 yards? If so, is this what was seen all week on film and an indication of coverage rotation? Safety depth, leverage, and location are the keys that unlock the coverage doors for the quarterback.

Next, the quarterback's eyes should go to the corners. Are the corners playing off, or are they pressed? Where are their eyes? Are they looking in the backfield, or are they looking at the receiver they are covering, indicating man-to-man coverage? After the quarterback checks the corners, he should come back and go front left to right, linebackers through to safeties, and corners left to right, and then make the appropriate decisions about what to do.

After hundreds of reps of assessing the defensive situation, the practice becomes routine and comfortable for the quarterback. Once he gets his routine established, his job is easier. Just like his footwork before throwing the football, his pre-snap routine is something that becomes a comfort mechanism for him. The more constant his routine, the more consistent he will become. If his eyes are all over the place before the ball is snapped, his chances for success will obviously lessen dramatically.

Before a play has a chance to succeed after the ball is snapped, the play has to be won before the snap. In order to achieve this objective, the quarterback has to know the situation. He has to know all of the variables of the situation. Once he knows them, he has to effectively communicate the appropriate information to his teammates. Whether a team huddles or it doesn't, this step has to happen flawlessly. Once this transfer of relevant information occurs, the quarterback needs to undertake a consistent routine of surveying the defense before the ball is snapped. If he does this consistently and effectively, because of his work in the film room, he will know what is getting ready to occur, before it actually does happen. When a quarterback is operating like that, he is operating at a championship level.

CHAPTER 7
Post-Snap Fundamentals

Not too many teams have their quarterback get under center anymore. Everyone is so shotgun-oriented that to see quarterbacks get under center has almost become a rarity. Nonetheless, the fundamentals of taking a snap can be an essential aspect of a quarterback's toolbox. Two schools of thought exist concerning the alignment of the quarterback's feet when he's under center.

❏ Taking a snap under center. Most of the pro-style offenses have gone to a slight stagger with the quarterback's feet. For a right-handed quarterback, that would mean that his left foot is staggered back to about the arch of his right foot or, at most, to his heel. The underlying rationale for such positioning is that on dropback passes of any sort or on any type of zone handoff, the stagger gives the quarterback a few inches head start that will enable him to get wherever he's going slightly faster.

The other way to go about it, which is the way I teach and personally prefer, is to have the quarterback's feet even when he's getting under center. In my opinion, the quarterback has better balance and can move more easily in all directions with his feet even. Furthermore, if he runs any type of option, he certainly is in a better and more balanced position, if his feet are square with each other.

When the quarterback gets up underneath the center, I tell him to get his feet aligned underneath his armpits, with his feet totally square. When the quarterback's feet are under his armpits, he is able to move in an athletic manner in all directions and still be completely balanced. Inexplicably, some quarterbacks get in such a wide stance that it gets them so sprawled out that they end up being in unbalanced and awkward places with their feet. In my opinion, having his feet under his armpits allows the quarterback to stand taller when he's under center, which provides him with the opportunity to see better.

I also tell my quarterbacks to slightly bend their knees and keep their back straight, while standing as tall as they can. There are a number of many quarterbacks who are tall, yet when they get in a staggered stance, with their knees bent a great deal, they figuratively become a short quarterback before the ball is snapped. In my opinion, quarterbacks should have a bend in their knees but stand as tall as possible, given that because doing so not only allows them to see better, it also enables them to make their pre-snap reads easier.

❏ The placement of the quarterback's hands under the butt of the center. How the quarterback places his hands under the center's butt is also an important post-snap fundamental for the quarterback. I want my quarterbacks to put the knuckle of their forefinger of their throwing hand right in the crack of the center's butt. Instead of placing their opposite hand directly underneath the right hand (if they are a right-handed quarterback), I tell them to put the big bones of their thumbs together.

Figure 7-1. Taking a snap

What the aforementioned positioning of the hands does is twofold. First, it slightly offsets the left hand, which is much more comfortable for the quarterback than having to bend his left arm in an uncomfortable position. More importantly, it allows the quarterback's elbows to have a little more bend. This bend allows for a natural "ride" of the center when he snaps the ball.

Arguably, over the years, a number of peewee foot coaches have advised their quarterback to "ride the center" when he snapped the ball. Not only is that unnatural, it slows him down. It also gets him up into the line too far. Furthermore, it can cause turnover problems if a guard is pulling.

As such, the quarterback should put the big bones of his thumbs together, i.e., put the pads of his thumbs together. Not only does such thumb placement allow him much more comfort, more importantly, it also enables him to have a natural "ride" with the center, because when he takes off, his elbows will slightly unbend, resulting in that natural ride. In reality, I've changed many quarterbacks over the years to this way of taking a snap. Frankly, not once have I heard one of them say that he liked it the other way better.

❏ Seat the ball. After the quarterback receives the ball from the center, the very first thing he has to do is "seat" the ball. What is "seat" the ball? When the quarterback seats the ball, he gets the snap and immediately brings the ball to his waist or belly button.

The quarterback must seat the ball before he does anything. If he doesn't, he is increasing the chances of putting the ball on the ground. If a snap from center is not seated, a pulling guard can knock the ball out of his hands, causing a turnover. A ball not seated can be knocked out of his hands by a running back, who doesn't have his elbow up properly.

❏ Put the weight on the inside ball of the foot opposite the direction he is going. The next fundamental after the quarterback seats the ball is whichever direction he is moving, he has to mentally put the weight on the inside ball of the foot opposite of the direction he is going. For example, if he is handing the ball off to his right, he must put his weight on the ball of his left foot, when pushing off. This action prevents false steps, which, in turn, not only precludes valuable lost time, it also averts timing problems, when the quarterback is executing a handoff, pitch, or pass.

If the quarterback is handing a ball off to a running back, he must seat the ball first. Then, he must drive off the leg opposite the side to which he is going. Next, he must drive the ball back and look the ball into the running back's pocket, an action that is referred to as "putting your head on the ball." The quarterback must put his head on the ball on every single handoff, or he is asking for a turnover.

❏ Handing the ball off. There are two schools of thought when handing a ball off. The first is to seat the ball and then show the ball the whole way to the running back. Once the quarterback gets to his running back, he either hands it off or sticks the ball in and pulls it out to fake. The underlying premise of this technique is to let everyone in the ball park see the ball and then let the deception be the handoff or fake. The other school of thought is to seat the ball, keep it seated so that no one can see the ball, and then either hand it off or execute the fake.

I've done both and like both. I tend to believe that there will be fewer balls on the ground by keeping the ball seated and having two hands on the ball for most of the time. In the first scenario, the quarterback, if he is going to his right, will keep the ball in his left hand, showing the ball the whole way. Then, he will either hand the ball off or put the ball in the running back's stomach, before pulling it out, if he is faking. In the second scenario, the quarterback will keep the ball seated and simply put his empty left hand out and put it in the running back's stomach while keeping the ball in his throwing hand if it's a fake. He will then let his left hand fly out, which facilitates the "now you see it, now you don't" part of the fake.

As previously discussed, over the years, I've seen a few footballs on the ground with the first way of faking, because the running back got his lead elbow up late, which knocked the ball out of the quarterback's hand. Regardless of which technique is utilized, when executing a handoff, the quarterback must let the hand that he hands off with fly away with the running back. He then needs to look back at the running back, before putting his hands together to execute the proper fake that goes with the play.

Personally, I prefer that when the quarterback is executing a naked or boot fake, he should let his hand fly off with the running back and glance back, almost looking over his hand or thumb. Meanwhile, his off hand is on his belt buckle. Once he finishes looking back, he should then put two hands together and sprint out the back end.

❏ Faking. A championship quarterback takes great pride in his fakes. He will become a master craftsman and critique himself diligently when watching film. The best quarterbacks I've been around have also been the best fakers, because of the great pride they take in everything that they do.

Fundamentals of Pitching the Ball on the Option

I am a big believer in that for a team to be a well-rounded offense, it needs at least one option in its arsenal. My opinions in this matter derive from the fact that when I sit and listen to defensive coaches devising all of their blitzes, if a threat of an option exists, they can't dial up all their blitzes they may have at their disposal, because some of them aren't sound against the option. To be sound against the option, the defense has to have people assigned to the running back, the quarterback, and the pitch. Obviously, they need to be sound in every single one of their blitzes or pressures against the option. If they aren't, they can be hurt badly at the most crucial of times.

❏ Pitching the football. My first 10 years in coaching were spent in an option offense. We ran what is now called the flexbone. In the process, I saw firsthand how to pitch the football. The way I recommend pitching a football is different than most everyone else. Frankly, I am different in a lot of ways to most coaches in many aspects of what is currently being taught. I am different in the stance I teach under center. I am different from most coaches concerning how I teach the handoff and fake. I am also different in how I teach a quarterback to pitch the football.

Most coaches refer to the option pitch as a thumbs-down pitch. This technique involves the quarterback holding the ball in the center of the ball and then pitching it with his thumb down as he actually pitches it. The way I teach the option pitch is for the quarterback to slightly slide his hand down the ball to a little past halfway and then pitch the ball, similar to shooting a basketball.

A number of advantages exist to pitching the ball basketball-style. First, the ball can be pitched much further basketball-style, than the thumbs-down version. Second, the pitch will have fewer rotations on the ball, making it easier to catch. Third, and most importantly, in wet weather, the ball never slips out of the quarterback's hand, like it sometimes does when pitching the ball thumbs down.

All factors considered, the basketball pitch makes it somewhat easier to coach the pitch back, given that he does not have to be concerned about being in a certain relationship with the quarterback. The standard pitch rule is 4x4 from the quarterback. With the basketball pitch, the coach can tell the pitch back to just haul butt, get flat, and run. This strategy allows him to get a couple of yards farther away from the quarterback, and, more importantly, a couple of yards farther away from the pursuit of the defense. The basketball pitch enhances the play of the quarterback, because he can pitch the ball further, with fewer rotations, and in wet weather.

Fundamentals of Throwing the Football

Underneath the Center

The next aspect of sound quarterback play to be discussed is the fundamentals of throwing the football from underneath the center. The first type of pass from under center to be covered is the three-step concept. Most every team has a three-step passing game.

A three-step passing game serves a number of purposes. First, it enables the offense to control the rush, because the ball is coming out so quickly and because a lot of teams use a cut protection when calling these routes. Personally, I like to cut defensive linemen when calling these routes, because it not only tends to slow down their rush, it also causes them, on occasion, to play tentatively throughout the game. Even if the blocker misses and turns somebody loose, I really like it, because of the four-quarter investment you are making by using some sort of cutting.

The other reason I like the three-step route structure is that it is such a high-percentage play. Three-step routes are particularly attractive on first-and-10 situations and on plays involving checks. These routes offer a desirable option when a team is coming out of its own end zone, as well as when it is in the red zone. The red zone is a great time to call these routes and incorporate some sort of check, because of all the pressures the offense tends to get in that area of the field.

The next aspect to be discussed regarding the fundamentals involved in throwing the ball when the quarterback is under center is a three-step drop for a right-handed quarterback, who is throwing to his right. In this instance, the quarterback is going to mentally put his weight on the inside ball of his left foot. The first step is key, because it is his depth step. He must get separation with his first step from the center. Even more importantly, he must get separation from the "big uglies" who are coming after him.

When the quarterback steps for depth, it is important that he not step "in the bucket." He needs to come straight back at 6 o'clock to get his maximum depth. His second step is a crossover step that should keep his shoulders perpendicular to the line of scrimmage. This step then becomes his "brake" step or the step on which he slows the momentum of his drop. On his third step, he should come to a complete stop, and then hit with a wide base, with his weight back.

The quarterback should be four to four and a half yards deep from the line of scrimmage. On most three-step drops from under center, when the quarterback hits on his third step, he should hit and throw. In reality, however, there are a few routes, for example, some shorter option routes by the tight end, or slant routes where he ends up throwing to a window, on which he doesn't hit on his third step and throw. I refer to this situation as one in which he will actually "hit and sit" as I call it. He will hit on his third step and sit on his back foot and wait for a split second for the route to develop.

A number of schools of thought exist concerning the three-step drop footwork when a right-handed quarterback is throwing to his left. As such, space is not available to review all of the different opinions and theories on this subject. Frankly, what I believe on this matter and teach has evolved over the years.

The main factor is to understand that the ball is coming out quickly, and the quarterback needs to help himself when throwing the ball to his left by somehow getting his hips more open to his target. His hips are extremely closed when throwing a short route to his left. In reality, his hips are completely opposite of his target, no matter what route has been called, when he's throwing to his left.

In order to help the quarterback get his hips going in the right direction, I require the quarterback to still use his first step as a separation step, but come out at almost a 45-degree angle to his right. This footwork will begin to open his hips to his target. The quarterback might not get quite as deep with his first step, but his hips will go from 90 degrees closed to his target to about 45 degrees.

The quarterback's second step will be at the same angle as his first step, which will open his hips even more to his target. His third step is a continuation of the first two. By the time he hits on his third step, his hips have become way more open to his target. As a consequence, he is subsequently capable of making a more accurate throw because of the footwork.

If the quarterback used the same footwork as a throw to his right, he would hit on his third step and just blindly swing his lead leg, hoping to get his hips open, yet making it very difficult to be consistent with either his step or his pass. More quarterbacks miss throws to their left than they do to their right. This situation occurs because they don't get open to their target. The point to remember is that the quarterback needs to step slightly to the left of his target to get his hips all the way open to his target.

When throwing to their left, quarterbacks who do not get their hips open, end up stepping at their target, instead of slightly to the left of their target. As a result, they end up throwing behind the receiver.

Figure 7-2. First step of three-step drop to the left

Figure 7-3. Third step of three-step drop to the left. Notice how open the quarterback's hips are.

Shotgun Stance

Similar to three-step drop footwork, the shotgun stance for a quarterback has many schools of thought. For example, one theory advocates that if a team is a zone read team and does all of the read concepts that many of the spread offenses do, the quarterback needs to have a square stance. In my opinion, if a team has any type of runs where the quarterback is asked to possibly be a runner, the square stance should be used. This stance is similar to being under center, only with the quarterback in a square stance. As a result, the quarterback is able to move in either direction with ease.

If the quarterback is throwing the football on a three-step route, he will take a small punch step with his left foot if he is a right-handed quarterback. This step should be no deeper than six inches and not more than three inches or so past his right foot. After he punches, his second step, with his right foot, should gain depth and his weight should be transferred just like if he were under center.

On most three-step routes from the gun, as the quarterback's second step hits, he should be ready to deliver the ball. Just as if he were under center, if he had a tight end option route or a second window slant or fade called, he would hit on his second step and then sit on his back foot until he was ready to deliver the ball.

With regard to the pure pro-style offenses, most of them prefer to have the quarterback's left foot staggered in a heel-toe relationship for the right-handed quarterback. Similar to the quarterback being under center, the underlying premise of this footwork technique is that it enables the quarterback to gain a few inches, when he's dropping back and throwing the football. When dropping back to pass with this staggered stance, the quarterback punch steps and then gains ground with his right foot, just as if he were in a square stance. Then, he either delivers the ball on his second step or hits and sits on his second step, depending on the route concept called.

❏ Five-step drops. Teams still do take five-step drops from under center. In reality, most of them play on Sundays. I love the five-step passing game for a number of reasons. For example, offenses can control the football with their first-, second-, and third-down throws. Furthermore, five-step drops provide teams with the ability to throw hot. These concepts also force the defense to defend the entire field. Personally, I like to utilize five-step routes on a variety of situations, including first down, on second-and-six or more, and on third-and-three or more yards. I have also found these concepts to be very effective in the red zone.

When taking a five-step drop from under center, the quarterback's weight should mentally be on the ball of his left foot for a right-handed quarterback. He should drive off the ball of his left foot. The first step with his right foot should be his depth step or separation step. Just like on the three-step drop, it is critical for the quarterback to gain separation from the line of scrimmage. His second step should be a crossover step.

The quarterback's third step should be another depth step. The quarterback needs to really reach, almost bound, with his third step to gain as much depth as possible. The fourth step, another crossover step, is, in reality a "brake" step. In other words, with this step, the quarterback is stopping all of his momentum and coming under control. As a result, when his fifth step hits the ground, it is down and solid. When the quarterback hits on his fifth step, he should have a wide base, and his weight should be back. Furthermore, he should be seven to seven and a half yards deep at the top of his drop.

On a five-step drop from the shotgun, the quarterback should punch step, roughly six inches with his left foot, just like he did on his three-step drop from the gun. He should then take three steps back. His first step with his right foot doesn't have to reach for depth, since he is already lined up five-yards deep. His second step should be a crossover-and-"brake" step. His third step should be put down, with a wide base and his weight back. At that point, he should be no deeper than eight yards from the line of scrimmage. Anything deeper than that puts him too deep in the pocket and in a direct line for those athletic defensive ends and outside linebackers who are pass rushing against the offensive tackles.

For the quarterback, the shotgun snap from center on a five-step drop is exactly the same as a three-step drop from under center. The keys to the drop are exactly the same except the quarterback doesn't have to reach for depth on his first step. The only difference in the gun is that it's catch and take three steps.

The primary point to remember is that the most efficient and most accurate quarterbacks have the most consistent drops. Inconsistent drops lead to inconsistent throws. Inconsistent drops lead to inconsistent mechanics when throwing the football. As discussed previously, the quarterback's footwork and mechanics are the keys to power, accuracy, and consistency. The best of the best have footwork like pistons. They drop the same way every time.

With the ever-evolving passing game and the growing sophistication of it, no one is claiming that some differences in some of the timing on some of the individual routes don't exist. They do. For example, some five-step drops from the gun might require a quick one, two, three, and throw. Furthermore, some deeper routes might require a catch and a quick one, two, three, four, five, shuffle, and throw.

For the most part, I believe that a team can take the basic five-step drop that was discussed previously and add a hitch or a shuffle step, after the quarterback hits on his fifth step to gain momentum and power before he throws, and have a wildly successful five-step passing attack. It should be noted that when a shuffle step is added after the quarterback hits on his fifth step, it is critical to make sure that when he takes his one shuffle step, that his feet don't come together, which would cause him to overstride.

Over the years, there have been a number of quarterbacks who take that shuffle step and get their feet so close together that they become "heel clickers." As a result, they overstride, leading to balls sailing or going in the dirt. A quarterback coach can't have his quarterback do too many drops during a practice. Any quarterback who wants to play at a championship level will do whatever it takes to become a consistent dropper.

In the 18 years that I have been an offensive coordinator, I have never had a seven-step drop. Frankly, I've never had good enough linemen to hold the defense out that long. Only one difference exists between a five-step drop and a seven-step drop. On a seven-step drop, the quarterback gains ground on steps one through five. The sixth step becomes the "brake" step, and the seventh step should be hit with a wide base and his weight back. At that point, his depth should be at nine-yards deep.

❑ Sprint-out passes. Sprint-out passes seem to have been around forever. Personally, I think that they are underutilized by many teams. In reality, sprinting out offers a number of advantages. For example, when training after sprinting out, the launch point of the ball is changed, which is always a good thing. To keep a quarterback in the same place for too long with the same launch point of the ball is only asking for trouble. The ability to attack the contain rusher and make him defend a multitude of different looks and blocks is another advantage. Sprinting out helps the offensive line, because the pocket has been moved. Finally, sprinting out allows the extension of route depths.

Any time the quarterback has been sacked or pressured is a good time to sprint out. Against teams who like to drop eight defenders into coverage is also a good time to sprint out and make some of those droppers become contain rushers, which creates more places to throw the ball.

If the quarterback is right-handed and is sprinting out to his right, he should mentally put his weight on the ball of his left foot. His first step should reach at a 45-degree angle and should work to get depth. By his third step, he should start working to get downhill. If the quarterback is sprinting out from under center, he shouldn't get deeper than seven yards. If he is throwing to his right, he will throw off his third, fifth, or seventh step. If he is throwing to his left, it will be on his fourth, sixth, or eighth step. If the quarterback is in the gun, the maximum depth he should ever reach would be nine yards.

The key to the sprint-out pass is for the quarterback to get his shoulders square to the target. As such, the quarterbacks should follow the ball. It is sometimes easier for a right-handed quarterback to get his shoulders squarer to his target when running to his left, than it is to his right.

If the quarterback is sprinting out to his right and doesn't get his right shoulder squared around to his target, there is a good chance that his ball is going to miss to the right. Conversely, if he is going to his left, his right shoulder has to come back and almost cock to the right in order for the ball not to sail to the left. As stated previously, a great coaching point is to have the quarterback "follow his ball." If he follows his ball, his shoulders will be in line with his target.

CHAPTER 8
Development Within the Passing Game

The quarterback in the game of football, as it currently exists, we now know it is the most important player on the team. Traditionally, a quarterback could be a manager of the game. Hand it off most of the time, throw it 10 to 14 times in a game, and all would be well. Not anymore. With the sophistication and evolution of the game on both sides of the ball, the quarterback has to play a significant role in every ballgame. One widely held precept, from the peewees to the pros, is that if a team doesn't have a good quarterback, it's hard to win a game, much less a championship.

A number of factors have come into play when devising a passing attack for the quarterback. In that regard, several musts that have to happen exist for the quarterback to develop into a championship caliber player. I employ the following checklist, which I check and recheck every year. The quarterback has to have these points ingrained in his mind, so that he can fully develop into the type of player he needs to be. This checklist, which has evolved over the years, has become fairly universal in nature. Certainly, the factors apply to every great offense of which I have been a part.

- Play to the strengths of the team and its personnel.
- Must throw completions.
- Need to be a good four-vertical team.
- Don't be greedy; dump it down.
- Rhythm, rhythm, rhythm.
- Make sure that the quarterback knows what he is facing defensively.

- Must be able to stretch the field, both vertically and horizontally.
- Must be able to properly time his progression reads.

❏ Play to the strengths of the team and its personnel. Every great coach and every great quarterback will play to the strength of their personnel. A quarterback will learn as he goes through his journey that playing favorites and trying to throw it to buddies will get his team beat. A quarterback is an extension of the coach, and, as such, he has to understand that personnel is a big key in winning.

The quarterback has to know who his best drive blocker is and who his best pulling offensive lineman. He has to know who is the toughest and who is the smartest blocker. All of these things matter when the game is on the line.

Perhaps the quarterback has to audible at the line of scrimmage on the biggest play of the year. If it's a run play, every variable that has been discussed will come into play. In a fraction of a second, the quarterback will have to make a check that will win or lose the game and maybe even a championship. His knowledge of his personnel and playing to the strengths of his personnel enhance the likelihood that he will make the right audible and run to his strength.

The same factor applies to the running backs and wide receivers. The quarterback has to know which receiver can get off press coverage. He has to know which receiver has the best feel for getting open against zone coverage. He has to know which of his receivers will go up and get a ball in the toughest of circumstances. When it's fourth-and-one on the goal line, which running back will find a way to get the ball in the end zone?

All of these questions are personnel-related. As such, all of them have to be answered if the goal of the quarterback is to play to the strengths of his personnel. All of these questions can be answered over the course of all the hours of film study and practice sessions. Furthermore, they all have to be answered at the moment of truth. Any good coach, if any question exists about what needs to be done, should respond by playing to the strengths of the players and the team.

I get asked all the time by offensive linemen about how much they should weigh. My first question is always, what is his biggest strength? If he says quickness, I will tell him that when in question, report to camp lighter, in order to be able to play to his strength. If he replies that strength and blocking are his biggest assets, I tell him not to worry too much about his weight, if it's within reason. In fact, every position group and every player needs to have great self-awareness about their biggest strengths, as well as work hard to improve their greatest weaknesses. The same factor applies to the offense as a whole. Every coach, particularly one who is a play caller, needs to understand and play to the strengths of his players and his team. The quarterback is in charge of all of this. He, above everyone else, has to understand not only his biggest strength, but the strengths of every player on the whole offense. If he has a great understanding of these strengths and plays to all of them, he will be well on his way to being able to compete like he wants to, needs to, and should.

❏ Must throw completions. Accuracy is the number one trait for a quarterback who plays in a balanced offense. The bottom line is that completions have to be thrown. Quarterbacks tend to be a confident group. Within the context of that confidence, many quarterbacks love to show off their big strong arm. Inexplicably, a number of young quarterbacks will throw the ball deep on the much lesser chance of a completion than throwing a shorter route that has a much higher chance of completion.

The quarterback needs to learn very early in the training process that when in doubt, he should throw the shorter pass. Completions keep the offense in manageable down-and-distance situations. For example, second-and-four is much better than second-and-10. Completions keep the offense on the field, as well as keep drives alive. All factors considered, if a quarterback throws enough completions, it will eventually lead to touchdowns and wins.

A quarterback who continues to push the ball down the field, when he has other completion opportunities much closer, is selfish. If a quarterback continues to exhibit such a tendency, he needs to be put on the bench. These types of quarterbacks care more about themselves than they do their team. A great quarterback cares about his team first. A quarterback needs to be taught very early in the developmental process that in order to start and play, he needs to, when in doubt, throw it short.

A quarterback who throws completions keeps his offense on the field and his defense off the field. Throwing completions is also a great source of frustration for the defense. An accurate quarterback who has the patience to throw the ball on a shorter route will cause defenses to start pressing, because their defense can't get off the field. It becomes almost like a great rushing attack in that no matter what the defense dials up, the defenders' efforts don't work.

Possession passing attacks have almost become like great rushing attacks. The ball that gets thrown five to six yards down the field by an accurate quarterback is almost like handing the ball off to a running back. Great possession passing teams can sustain drives, like great rushing teams, because of the accuracy of the quarterback and his willingness to take what the defense is giving him.

An accurate quarterback is a must. Furthermore, an accurate quarterback who chooses to throw completions makes for a dynamic and consistent offense. A quarterback who is inaccurate and not willing to throw the ball short leads to inconsistent offensive play and inconsistent offenses in general.

❏ Need to be a good four-vertical team. Being a good four vertical team can set the table for a highly diversified passing attack. It enables the offense to make the defense have to defend the entire field. It creates a fear factor within a defense, because of the offense's ability to push the ball vertically, with four receivers running as fast as they can down the field. It also puts tremendous pressure on everyone involved in pass coverage. If a team can become good at throwing four verticals, it opens up everything underneath and allows the offense to attack at will when throwing the football.

Four verticals put the outside receivers in an area that is usually the numbers on the football field. It puts the inside receivers on or close to the hash marks on the field. If this situation is the rule, a team can be very multiple in its alignments and formations when attacking with this route. It can align with two receivers on either side of the ball or with three receivers on one side and one on the other. From a formation standpoint, the possibilities are endless. If the quarterback has a great feel for throwing four verticals, the multiplicity within that capability creates a veritable nightmare for the defense to defend.

Throwing four verticals does not necessitate throwing the ball 50 yards down the field. It is a timing throw, just like most other passes in an offense. The quarterback must know that when throwing to one of his inside receivers running up the seam, that the magic spot for throwing the ball is 18 to 22 yards. Anything deeper, the safety will either blow the receiver up or can intercept the ball. When working these routes, the quarterback has to understand that this concept is all about timing and has nothing to do with arm strength.

The ability to throw four verticals can be learned and taught. If mastered by your quarterback, the four verticals concept can make a team so much harder to defend. When taking drops, whether under center or in the shotgun, the quarterback needs to understand that he needs to cut his drop just enough so when he hits on his last step, he is ready to deliver the ball. He needs to know that on an inside seam, when the receiver is even with the underneath coverage defender, he needs to let the ball go. If the quarterback waits until his receiver clears the underneath coverage, it will be too late to throw the ball, possibly resulting in an interception.

If the ball goes to an outside receiver, the quarterback needs to understand what his coverage is. Against cover 2, he has to know to throw it in the hole between the safety and the corner on a line. If it's single coverage, and the corner is on top of his receiver, and his eyes are on the receiver, it's a great opportunity to throw it to the back shoulder of the receiver. If the receiver is running past the defensive back, it is important that the quarterback not throw it to the receiver. Rather, he should throw the ball four yards from the sideline and allow his receiver to get on top of his defender, and let the ball take him to his spot.

It's easy to understand why the ability to throw four verticals is so beneficial for your quarterback to be good at and for your offense to be able to execute, when you listen to defensive coaches talk about it. There is nothing worse than for a defensive back to give up a big play, when he's being attacked vertically. As an offensive coach at practice, it's easy to see how much it stresses both defenders and defensive coaches, because of all the time invested in working on defending the play. When the amount of practice time spent on defending the play and the fear of all defensive backs of giving up a "big one" are combined, it's understandable how significant this concept can be to a quarterback and an offense. For an offense to reach its full potential and for a quarterback to reach his full potential, a significant effort should be expended on mastering the ability to throw four verticals.

❏ Don't be greedy; dump it down. A great quarterback is like a surgeon. He will slice you up bit by bit. He won't be concerned about stats or showing off his arm. He is concerned about throwing completions and getting the ball down the field into the end zone.

The really good quarterbacks are not greedy. They will dump the ball down to their shortest outlet all day long. As such, there needs to be a lot of time spent on teaching the quarterback where his check-down route is and who it is.

In that regard, we do something different from most people, which I really like. Once a year in a pass skeleton drill, I tell our quarterback to only throw the ball to our check-down. If there are 20 plays in this particular pass skeleton session, we check it down 20 times.

After a while, the defense may start playing the drill, but that's okay. The objective is for the quarterback to have a complete understanding of who and where his check down is. Conducting the drill in this manner also reinforces how important it is to dump the ball down. It forces everybody to buy in to the fact of not being greedy and reinforces to whoever is running the check-down route that he better work to get open, because he may very well get the ball.

On a number of occasions, the check-down route receiver is a running back. This drill should reinforce to him that just because he hasn't gotten the ball the last five times that this route has been called, that it isn't going to happen the next time. In reality, every receiver on every route needs to expect the ball. If he is playing with a quarterback who has great vision, he can get the ball on any route at any time.

A number of statistics exist, especially in the NFL, that show a percentage of how many balls are thrown down the field. They report the percentages of passes from 0 to 10, 10 to 20, etc. In fact, the most successful quarterbacks in the game throw an insane percentage of the time in the range of 0 to 10 yards.

What does this say? It indicates that the greatest quarterbacks in the game of football are not selfish. It reflects the fact that they understand that the object is to get first downs and sustain drives, which leads to points. It points out that they aren't greedy. They will dump the ball down all day long. Surely, if the great quarterbacks in the game can have that mentality, then coaches can work with their quarterbacks to have the same mindset.

❏ Rhythm, rhythm, rhythm. The most consistent passing attacks are those in which the ball is thrown on time. The route depths marry up with the drop of the quarterback. The receiver must have great discipline in his route running, as well as in his route depths. If a receiver runs too far or cuts his route off too short, the quarterback will miss his throw a good amount of the time. Likewise, if a quarterback takes a seven-step drop on a five-step route, the timing of the route will be screwed up. As a consequence, the ball will get there late, resulting in possible incompletions and even worse, interceptions.

The timing of the passing game is everything, and it is all about rhythm. Some of the best times to work on rhythm are when just the quarterbacks and receivers go out and throw by themselves. This effort could be undertaken any time they both have some free time in the off-season. All factors considered, the summer months are the best time to work on their chemistry and timing, because the weather is good. Furthermore, the effort should have great carryover to the season, which is imminent.

During football season, there should never be a day go by that the quarterbacks and receivers don't get together and throw routes, before they ever get to any group work against the defense. This effort needs to be a particular emphasis at every practice. Furthermore, it needs to be monitored and executed at a high level.

Poor throws by the quarterback and poor routes and drops by the receivers should not be tolerated. Very few balls should hit the ground during these periods, if a team plans on having a successful passing attack. Every time the quarterback throws to his receivers, the timing and trust should increase. If a bunch of balls hit the ground, for one reason or another, the chances of success in team situations drop dramatically.

Quarterbacks will learn that on an out route, for example, that the ball needs to be thrown when the receiver plants his feet to get on his out, before he ever looks for the ball. Receivers will understand that when they come out of their break on the out cut, that the ball will already be in the air. As a result, they need to be ready for the ball to be on top of them.

The best passing games are those in which everyone works in complete unison. It is almost like synchronized swimming. Everyone has to be exactly where he is supposed to be and everything has to be locked in to the imaginary clock in his head, because the quarterback understands that he controls the timing of the passing game.

When the quarterback is ready to throw, the ball needs to come out. If a receiver is getting pressed, it's the responsibility of the receiver to get off the line and get into his route. Otherwise, he is not getting the ball, and he is certainly not getting it when he wants it.

The best passing games are those in which, when the quarterbacks and receivers are working together, they rarely allow a ball to hit the ground. When it's time to conduct a pass skeleton drill, the quarterback's completion percentage should be upwards of 90 percent. Is this level of achievement going to happen every time? Probably not, but the vast majority of time, the completion percentage should be very high.

In all likelihood, if a team's offensive unit is not completing 85 to 90 percent of their passes in pass skeleton drills, its passing game isn't going to be great. Why? Because there are no defensive linemen or linebackers rushing the quarterback; there isn't the chaos happening in front of the quarterback that occurs in a game. The quarterback always has a throwing lane, and in the back of his mind, he knows that he will have time to make the throw.

In some ways, pass skeleton or 7-on-7 exercises are some of the best drills for the quarterback. In turn, in some ways, they aren't very relevant to the game itself. They can be great for the rhythm of the passing game, as well as productive for him to see all of the coverages that will come his way during the week. On the other hand, because there isn't "glass breaking" in front of the quarterback, they aren't very realistic on occasion.

In reality, every team that practices the game of football employs pass skeleton drills. Personally, while I like the drills, coaches need to emphasize that the percentage of balls completed during these drills should be very high, as well as the fact that there must be plenty of team passing drills done during the week.

These team drills should consist of team blitz pick-up and team pass activities, which mostly involve coverage, as opposed to having pressure coming. To have an effective passing attack, the rhythm part must be practiced in situations in which it is the most difficult for both the quarterback and the receivers. As a rule, those situations tend to best occur during 11-on-11 drills.

It cannot be emphasized too much that the quarterback must control the timing of the passing game. No one else can control it, but him. On occasion, receivers will try to control the timing of the passing game by not running their routes at full speed or by not practicing with the sense of urgency that the quarterback does. When this situation occurs, it must be corrected.

The best passing games get honed when the receivers work just like the quarterback does. Game-day preparation and game-day speed. Whether it's an effort issue or another factor, like receivers being rerouted, when receivers start to dictate the timing of the throws, the quarterback's completion percentages start to drop dramatically. I ask my quarterbacks all the time to throw the ball when they are ready. Don't wait for the receiver to get open.

If the quarterback is back in the pocket, holding the ball, waiting to throw it, there's a big problem. If that situation exists, a team might require some new receivers, who need a shot to play. If a receiver is getting pressed, he should get off and get vertical. If a receiver has an in cut at 15 yards, he should get to 15 as fast as possible and work to get open.

The quarterback has to control the timing of the passing game. Everyone must be aware of this factor and be on the same page. Your quarterback cannot compromise on this concept, which is where some of the coaching that I talked about previously applies.

Every time a timing issue occurs, the quarterback has to address it and make it known that he is ready to throw the ball. Furthermore, if the receiver wants to catch the ball, he needs to get to where he is supposed to be. If the receivers don't get the ball thrown their way enough and when they hear about it enough, it won't take them too long to understand if they want to play, they will run with a sense of urgency, practice with a sense of urgency, and compete with a sense of urgency on every play of every practice and game. When this scenario occurs, the timing of a team's passing game can take off.

❏ Make sure that the quarterback knows what he is facing defensively. While this factor is obvious. It is worth emphasizing. The quarterback must know what he is getting defensively every play. If a quarterback is ever fooled with a front, blitz, or coverage, the chances for success of the play diminish to almost nothing.

The knowledge that the quarterback needs to have, in this regard, is derived from hours of film study during the week. It is also a by-product of performing walk-throughs before practice, as well as engaging in the full speed practice that follows. A quarterback should be the first player in after a game to watch his performance. Once that is over, he should start his film study of his next opponent. Film study is of utmost importance. As a rule, the best quarterbacks do it with more frequency and at a much higher level than the average ones do. After your quarterback has initially grasped an understanding of what is being seen on the tape, he can then apply that information to a physical reality by walking through and then practicing the appropriate technique or skill.

A quarterback needs to be able to know what is coming before the snap. This knowledge enables him to also be aware of what he is doing either in his run-checks or what and how he is going to progress his throws in the passing game. A quarterback who knows exactly what he is getting (defensively) before the ball is snapped is going to have a much higher success rate than the quarterback who is guessing.

The quarterback who can process all this information before the snap can attack with confidence. A quarterback who has a great idea of what is getting ready to happen before the ball is snapped has a much higher degree of success, because of the knowledge he gained through his game preparation. A quarterback who knows what he is getting defensively is a quarterback who is going to win.

❏ Must be able to stretch the field, both vertically and horizontally. The quarterback has to understand the tactical principles of throwing the football. He has to understand why and how offenses attack defenses. When throwing the football, defenders have to be stretched both vertically and horizontally. This scenario puts the defender in a bind, both in front and in back of him, as well as on both sides of him. Hypothetically, if a triangle is envisioned, that's how a team needs to design its dropback passing game. Creating triangles in the passing game places the maximum amount of pressure possible on a defense.

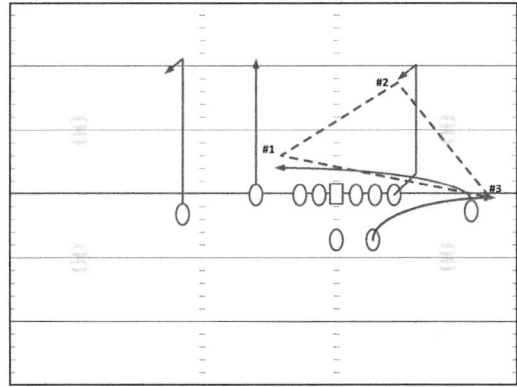

Figure 8-1. Triangle example A

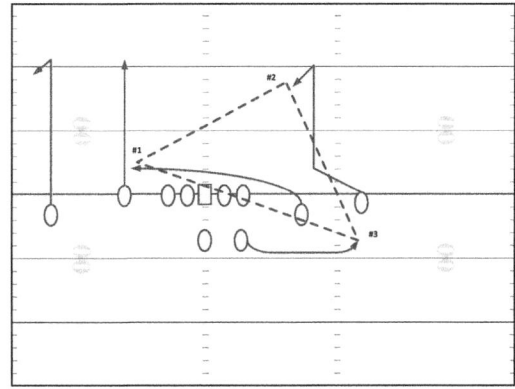

Figure 8-2. Triangle example B

When the field is stretched both vertically and horizontally, the quarterback can take his focus off of reading particular defenders and can then focus on going from one receiver to the next. When triangles are created, the quarterback can progress from receiver #1 to #2 to #3. These triangles are built by positioning different receivers in relatively the same spots. In reality, the same routes can be run in many different ways by either changing the formation or interchanging the routes of the receivers.

As a result, the exact same route can have many different looks by doing the aforementioned. Even though it is the same route to the quarterback, it has the appearance of many different routes when the opponent is breaking down the offense. If the quarterback understands this concept, it not only helps his growth as a player, it also enhances his ability to contribute ideas within each game plan.

❏ Must be able to properly time his progression reads. In developing the quarterback from being able to read defenders to going through progressions, he needs to have an understanding of the timing involved. For example, the quarterback can't hang on one receiver too long, or it will make him late to his next progression. Conversely, if the quarterback passes through one read too fast, it makes him early to his next look.

If a clock was somehow magically put on a quarterback, it would probably find that quality quarterbacks tend to spend between .4 and .8 of a second on each progression. This factor has to be learned. Furthermore, it has to be coached and watched on every play of every practice.

Once the quarterback masters the progression read, a whole new world of possibilities are opened up to him, with regard to the ability to create a multitude of routes. Triangles can be built coming from the opposite side of the field, as well as be created on multiple levels.

It is important to note that the point is not being made that more routes make the offense better. Personally, I believe that less is more. More routes don't make the offense better. In reality, better execution makes the offense better.

Another aspect of progression reads is triangles. As such, progressions can be created across the entire football field. Unless the quarterback plays in the NFL, there are very few quarterbacks under that competitive level who can actually do a great job with full-field progressions. As I stated previously, I believe that less is more. In turn, if the quarterback is a junior high, high school, or even college quarterback, I would discourage the use of full-field progressions as a major component of a team's passing game. Rather, I encourage the use of half-field reads, a technique in which the quarterback only works a triangle on either the right side or the left side of the field. While a receiver can come from the opposite side of the field to create the triangle, we only work half the field the vast majority of the time.

In reality, very few quarterbacks can truly execute full-field progressions at a very high competitive level. In that same vein, only a special quarterback can consistently get past his third progression. As such, the vast majority of good passing offenses employ progression reads.

If a quarterback coach was totally honest, he would be aware of the fact that there are not that many quarterbacks who can consistently go all the way from his first progression to his third, and still be great at it. If the quarterback can get all the way through and truly be looking at what he is supposed to look at and not passing through his reads too quick, he is well on his way to being special. In the more than two decades that I have been coaching quarterbacks, only a handful have truly been excellent at completing all of their reads. If a fourth or fifth progression was added to their reads, those numbers would dwindle even more. There is simply not enough time to master getting to a fourth or fifth progression. In reality, most quarterbacks don't have a great enough feel for the game to be able to execute that level of reads.

The best ways to simulate progression reads in practice are to practice making the quarterback take his drop and then go through each route with his eyes and feet. His feet should tell the coach where the quarterback's progression is. For example, if a quarterback has a curl route to his right, once the last step of the drop is taken, his feet should open to his curl, and his lead shoulder should be on the target. After that, if his next progression is to his back in the flat, his feet should open to his back. Besides actually doing it in pass skeleton drills or live, this approach is the best way to get the clock in his head ticking, with an understanding of the feel it takes go from one read to the next.

Pass skeleton drills are great tools, because not only can the coach go through each route, the quarterback gets a feel for the time spent on each progression. Furthermore, the coach can incorporate blitzes to make the quarterback show who his hot receiver is or who his blitz control route is.

Practice time should be spent each day with just the coach and the quarterback going through drops and reads against air. These periods, which are invaluable, can enhance the quarterback's understanding not only of the timing involved, but also the schematics involved. The ability for the quarterback to be able to stretch the field both vertically and horizontally can put the defense in a substantial bind. It also opens up a whole new world of possibilities for route structure. The championship quarterback will become a master of going through his reads. His ability to go from progressive read #1 to #2 to #3 will become an integral part of him on his quest to achieve greatness.

CHAPTER 9
How to Watch Film

A huge difference exists between watching film and studying film. The vast majority of players who come in and watch film do just that. They watch the film, like they are watching a movie or a TV sitcom. They see what unfolds on the film, but don't look for the details that need to be learned in order to help them gain an advantage over their opponent in the next game.

The quarterback has to be concerned with every element of the defense and its personnel. As such, he needs to be taught the depths of how to watch film and shown how to better gain an advantage through film study. Once the quarterback understands how to watch film, a whole new world opens up to him. It is also just one more way for him to become another coach on the field.

A quarterback who is equipped with the knowledge of how to watch film has added another weapon to his arsenal. A quarterback, who knows how to properly glean the information that is available to him in the film room, can learn what the defense is about to do before they ever do it. That knowledge can provide substantial comfort to the quarterback on game day. The confidence that can be gained through proper film study helps the quarterback go into every contest with great confidence that he and his teammates have a huge advantage and will ultimately find a way to win.

Defenses have tendencies, just like offenses do. Despite what most individuals think, good teams have tendencies, no matter how hard they are tried to be covered up. For example, if the defense is running a twist stunt in their defensive line, a particular defensive lineman may give a tip that something is about to occur, before the stunt is executed. It might be a change in stance by one of the interior tackles. He may change which hand he puts down in his stance from his normal stance. He might be a player who normally lines up in a right-handed stance, but in order to move to get into his stunt, for example, he might put his left hand down to be able to move more efficiently to execute the stunt. If he doesn't change hands in his stance, he may tip off what he is about to do by putting less weight on his hand in his stance, before running that same stunt. His stance might go from a staggered stance to a square stance.

In another scenario, a linebacker, who normally lines up in the B gap, might move slightly to one side or the other to better put himself in position to execute a blitz that might be called. Linebackers often move slightly to better place themselves in position to take care of either their gap responsibilities in the defense or the coverage that has been called on that particular play.

Safeties talk to the quarterback on virtually every play. If the safeties normally line up showing some sort of two-deep look, one safety or both can tell a quarterback if they are going to stay in a two-deep look, or if they are going to rotate to a single-safety look by either the depth of their alignments or their location. Corners can tell a story as well. On numerous occasions, corners who are going to play zone coverage will look in the offensive backfield, knowing they have no man-coverage responsibilities. Frequently, when corners are in man coverage, their eyes will go from the backfield to the man they are covering—the wide receiver.

Over the years, I have developed and refined a checklist for the quarterback to watch when he comes in and studies film on the next opponent. This list provides the quarterback with a viable guide not only in what to look for, but also in how to watch film. For obvious reasons, this checklist is more in-depth than checklists for players at other positions. The following list details some of the factors, with regard to the defense, that our quarterbacks are not only asked to watch for, but also to know and understand:

- What are the major fronts?
- What are their major coverages?
- Who are their force players?
- When and how do they blitz?
- How do they adjust to motion?
- Tips on coverage by linebackers
- Tips on coverage by defensive backs
- Best areas and individuals to run at
- Do they play a prevent-type defense?
- What are their top two coverages in a two-minute drill?
- Who are their substitutes and when?
- Do they flip-flop their safeties?
- Do they flip-flop their linebackers?

- Do they stem the front?
- What are our best screens and draws?
- What is the best area to run at in short-yardage and goal-line situations?
- What defensive back should we go at in a crucial situation?
- Are they vulnerable to reverses or special plays?
- What is their goal-line defense?
- Who and what are their blitz keys?

As can be seen, this list is extensive. It can't and shouldn't be filled out and learned in one or even two sittings. It takes time to study all of these factors, which is the inherent beauty of it. It forces the quarterback to look at specific aspects of the opponent that are both personnel-related and structure-related.

Some factors are better addressed earlier in the week, while others can be left for later in the week. For example, the offense must understand early what the defense's base fronts and coverages are. Blitz keys and whom the offense should pick on should also be looked for early in the film study.

On the other hand, factors like what the offense does in prevent situations and two-minute situations can be determined later in the week, because they probably won't be practiced until Thursday anyway. Tips by down linemen and linebackers in their stances and locations need to be looked at early, given that the quarterback is studying what the base fronts and coverages of the defense are.

When the defense does something besides their base, it's helpful to start looking for tips, based on some of the factors outlined in the checklist. While it's normal to study film and start dreaming up what plays might work against the defense that week, teams need to understand that the structure and personnel of the defense are what's important early in the process.

There are a number of factors that we like to look at, as we go through the week with our quarterback. Do all of them get answered on the list each week? On occasion, they don't. For example, there may not have been a two-minute situation that has come up, because it's early in the year. For the most part, however, all of the factors on the checklist can and should be addressed.

By giving the quarterback a checklist to look for and to fill out, he has been equipped to better understand how to watch the film. As a rule, as the week progresses, the coaches study the tape to no end. As a result, when the quarterback comes in for the regular quarterback meetings, he can then understand why certain plays have been put in and why. As he gets more comfortable, he can even make suggestions concerning what might work against the opponent that week.

We also like our quarterback to answer some other broader questions concerning the game plan. Questions that we, as coaches, tend to ask and go through each week involve issues, insights, and situations that the quarterback should be fully aware of as well. These questions tend to be more game-plan oriented, as opposed to scheme-, structure-, and personnel-related. In that regard, the checklist we utilize includes the following queries:

- How did teams make big plays?
- How can we run the ball effectively?
- How do we attack with play action passes?
- What is their bunch adjustment?
- What formation do they defend the best and the worst?
- Have they seen an unbalanced formation? Are they sound in alignment?
- What are their answers to empty?
- Can we gain an advantage by putting the formation in to the boundary?
- How much do they change game to game?
- Do they show different looks after the first half?
- How do they react after a touchdown?
- Do they have injuries that can affect the game?

As quarterbacks begin their journey into the world of film study, most of them like for their coach to be with them to help guide them through the first few times. As they get more comfortable, they are able to do it on their own and actually begin to like to do it on their own, which is good, because it helps generate more individual thoughts and ideas. On occasion, coaches can get in a rut when it comes to developing game plans and utilizing the quarterback.

If he's taught properly, the quarterback can begin to add his own thoughts and ideas into the plan. When the quarterback begins to help more with the game plan, he has more ownership of the offense, which leads him to take an even keener interest in what is being implemented that week. The quarterback may begin to suggest plays with which he is most comfortable with and likes the most, especially in the passing game.

Subsequently, it will become easier to recognize whom the quarterback thinks his best receivers are. In turn, his coach will become more aware of whom his quarterback thinks his go- to running backs are, as well as whom he feels his best offensive linemen are. Furthermore, when the quarterback begins to understand everything involved with film study of his opponent, there won't be a week that goes by when he doesn't offer a great idea or see something critical that the coaches have missed. Not only will another crucial set of eyes and ideas be gained, a whole other level of understanding and trust will begin to emerge in the relationship between the coach and the quarterback.

Typically, on Thursday, we have the game plan typed up and ready to go, with all of the first- and second-down calls. Every third-down-and-distance situation, in addition to every other scenario imaginable, will be addressed on that call sheet. As his coach, I go through every call in every situation with the quarterback. If there happens to be a call on the sheet that he is not comfortable with, in most cases, it will get erased. If he has a different or better call in mind for a particular situation, I will usually make the change.

The primary advantage of meeting with the quarterbacks on the call sheet is that no surprises occur on either end come game day. On occasion, the coach may be surprised that the quarterback doesn't like a certain play, for whatever reason. After the calls are discussed and vetted, a decision will be made to either keep the play or throw it out. It is important to note, as his coach, that there will be times when no matter how much your quarterback isn't crazy about a call, if you know in your gut that it is something that will work, he needs to get over it and make it work.

Watching film and studying film are two entirely different things. The best-of-the-best quarterbacks take great pride in their film study and work ethic within the process of studying film. The ability to focus on the little things that can be observed during film study, like stances, alignments, eyes, and feet, is essential for every quarterback who wants to become good at his craft. The quarterback who can be taught how to study film and then will follow through with it every week provides his team with a great opportunity to win every time it takes the field.

CHAPTER 10
Situational Football

Football has become a game of situations. Whether it is third down backs, who come in the game for protection or receiving purposes, or a fifth defensive back, who comes into the game defensively for coverage purposes, the game has evolved to a game of situational football. As such, the quarterback needs to become a master of situational football. He needs to understand what the situation is and be able to execute within whatever situation exists at a particular moment in the game.

Every situation is a game within a game. Usually, whichever team wins the most situations, has a great opportunity to eventually win the game. Time and again, it has been documented that whatever team wins the turnover battle, and whatever team has more explosive plays than its opponent wins the game the vast majority of the time.

On numerous occasions, a game will come down to a goal-line stand or an overtime period. As such, every team must practice these situations and devote time to working on all the different scenarios. Many times, whichever quarterback executes the best in the given situation, will be on the team that wins.

Almost every situation that is addressed in this chapter is a scenario that needs to be practiced and scrimmaged during training camp. These situations need to be talked through and practiced every week to make sure the team, especially the quarterback, understands what has to occur in order to achieve the desired outcome. Among the offensive situations covered in this chapter are the following:

- Coming out
- Third down
- Red zone
- Goal line
- Four-minute
- Two-minute
- Last play of the game
- Overtime

❏ **Coming out.** One of the most challenging situations in all of football is for a team to bring the ball off of its own goal line. To be backed up on its own one-yard line, typically, with countless loud and crazy fans right behind a team, can be an intimidating proposition if the scenario hasn't been practiced and rehearsed over and over. Training camp is a great time for a team to practice its coming-out offense.

This situation is a set of circumstances that needs to be scrimmaged to have the appropriate impact on the players on offense, especially the quarterback. The quarterback has to know that his goal is to not turn the football over, but rather to get one first down. The underlying objective is not a 99-yard drive. Although such a drive would be nice and certainly is a possibility, the goal is to get the ball off of the goal line, so that the punter isn't backed up to the end line when he has to punt.

When the punter is backed up to the end line, he does not have a full 15 yards to work with to punt the ball. Obviously, that means the defensive rush is closer. As a result, the threat of a blocked kick is much greater. The other problem is that the punter has his heels as far back as he can to the end line. As such, an errant snap of any kind that makes him adjust his feet can result in him stepping out of the end zone, which means an automatic safety. Not only is giving up two points bad, but the resulting possession is lost, because the ball has to be punted.

As noted, the quarterback has to understand that his main focus is simply to take care of the ball and get one first down. The quarterback should also be aware that this is a great time to change the cadence to try and make the defense jump offsides and get a cheap first down. When this scenario occurs, it is the result of good coaching, and even better quarterback play.

To get a first down in that situation is not only great for the offense, it also has a tendency to take a little bit of juice out of the defense. Taking care of the ball also entails that every snap from under center has to be ensured by the quarterback. In addition, every handoff to a running back should be looked in by the quarterback and should involve the quarterback putting his "head on the ball." A number of head coaches won't let their offensive coordinator pitch the ball on an option because of the fear of an errant pitch or turnover.

The situation also mandates that when a pass play is called, it is critical that the pass is completed. Furthermore, when in doubt, the quarterback should throw the ball short, in order to maximize the potential of a completion. A turnover down in this area of the field is almost guaranteed to result in a touchdown for the opponent. Furthermore, not gaining a first down in this scenario greatly increases the odds that the opponent will score points of some sort, because of the field position the opponent achieves.

The main point that needs to be emphasized is that the quarterback has to execute flawlessly and know and understand the big picture when his team is on its own goal line. The big picture is simply to get a first down. If that scenario occurs, the situation has been won. Is the team out of the woods because it made a first down? No, but the punter is not punting in the shadow of his own end zone. The opponent wasn't given an easy score or handed a safety. The offense has gained valuable field position, which makes it somewhat more difficult for the opponent's offense to score, as opposed to having to punt in the next few downs.

Knowledge of the situation and knowledge of the goal of the offense is a must for the quarterback. Another appropriate time to practice being backed up is on Thursday. The offense and the quarterback should know what three calls will be made when they're coming off the goal line. When the situation is practiced every week, the task doesn't seem as daunting for anyone, especially the quarterback. Comfort is gained not only in knowing what call is coming in, but also by practicing these calls against the anticipated defensive looks. Coming-out offense is an important situation. If it is practiced and understood by the quarterback, the odds that success will occur will increase dramatically.

❏ Third down. Third down has become a game within the game itself. Over the years, most defensive coaches have expanded their team's third down packages to include different schemes than they use on first and second down. In fact, a number of defensive coordinators develop exotic blitz packages for their squads to employ on third down. Furthermore, defensive coordinators, if they base out of a four-down-linemen package, will often go to a three-down front. The underlying premise is to cause confusion among the offensive linemen in pass protection. A combination of exotic pressures and different defensive fronts can make it an extremely difficult down for the offense to navigate.

The quarterback has to know how the coaching staff feels about each down-and-distance scenario. The quarterback is already aware of what the various third down calls are for every different down-and-distance situation. He also has to know how to play the down and distance from a coach's perspective.

If the quarterback has a route structure on third-and-seven, he needs to understand that if he has a post and a dig combination, he doesn't have to throw the post to get the first down. In fact, he really needs to give the dig every opportunity to come open, because that is the route that is the higher percentage completion possibility. Every third down situation has to be learned to be played by the quarterback in conjunction with the coach's feelings on the play, which is the way to execute the play that gives the offense its best chance to convert.

A number of different ways exist to break third down up as a playcaller. What method is ultimately chosen is strictly based on a personal and philosophical basis from the staff's standpoint. The third down breakdown that I prefer is as follows:

- Third-and-one
- Third-and-two to -three
- Third-and-four to -six

- Third-and-seven to -eight
- Third-and-9 to -11
- Third-and-12-plus

Third-and-one is obviously a situation on which the offense should get a high percentage of first downs. It is a down on which most teams will try to run the football, unless the offense is close to the red zone and wants to take a shot, knowing they can come back and get the first down on fourth down. In this down-and-distance situation, if an offense can't get a first down by running the football, it could be argued, in many instances, that they don't really deserve to win the football game anyway.

The quarterback has to have a can-do attitude when he's verbalizing the play to his teammates. He should have great confidence in the call coming in, as well as great confidence in the ability of his teammates to execute the call. This situation is another appropriate time to teach the quarterback that this is a fitting scenario to change the cadence to try and make the defense jump offsides to get a cheap first down.

Defensive coordinators have different philosophies concerning third-and-one situations. Some coordinators will play base defense, almost conceding the first down, in order not to give up a cheap score or a big play. Other coordinators sell out, with stunts and blitzes and man coverage, trying to force the punt.

On numerous occasions, deciding what to do comes down to where the game is with regard to the time left on the clock and the score of the game. The quarterback needs to understand these various factors in order to give his offense its best chance for success. In reality, third-and-one is a down that the offense should convert a big percentage of the time, if it's worth a hoot.

Third-and-two to -three is a down that still is in the favor of the offense, but it has changed over the years. Up until the last few years, this particular down and distance situation was still mostly run-oriented. In the last few years, a number of people are viewing third-and-three as a pass down. In fact, in the NFL, it seems that third-and-two has become a pass down.

The quarterbacks should be taught that this down and distance is still a situation in which the offense is going to be tough and hard-nosed. Furthermore, the offense will often run the ball, perhaps more than most other teams tend to do.

The quarterback should be taught that, normally, defenses in this down-and-distance situation will become more multiple, will blitz, and will work really hard at getting a stop. Furthermore, the quarterback should understand that this is a great time to check to an option, if the defense wants to get too cute in what it is attempting to do. He should also be aware that he should incorporate some three-step routes, run-action passes, and a couple of five-step concepts into his playcalls in order to convert in this particular down and distance.

The quarterback also needs to be taught that any pass he throws doesn't have to go very far down the field in order to get to the sticks to move. Accordingly, if he's in doubt, he should throw the ball short and move on. In addition, the quarterback needs to be sure when he's checking to an option. He needs to know that he's checking into an option play that can really be effective against the defense he's facing, and possibly gain big yardage. The quarterback has to know that it is essential for him to take care of the football in these situations. As such, he must always see the pitch back clearly and make the pitch properly. The point to remember is that the quarterback must have a great handle on the various factors involved in situational football in order to maximize his team's chances to be successful.

Third-and-four to -six is a down-and-distance situation in which the defender's pressures, blitzes, and different fronts and stunts really show themselves. This particular down-and-distance scenario is one that has become almost a science project by some defensive coordinators, because of all the multiplicity involved. Over the years, this is a down-and-distance situation in which the chances of run have dramatically diminished. It is one in which the defensive coaches are often willing to roll the dice a little, with all of the different looks that they want to present. Typically, this down-and-distance situation is one that features higher blitz percentages across the board for all defensive coordinators.

In a third-and-four to -six situation, the quarterback has to be locked in and ready to change protections, and be ready to throw hot, as well as ready to max a protection. In reality, he has to be ready for anything. It is important that the quarterback understand that whatever route is called in this situation, it doesn't have to go past the sticks in order to convert. He has to understand that it's acceptable for him to throw the ball to a running back in the flat, if the back is open. All factors considered, it doesn't take long to cover five yards. Even if a defender gets there before the back, the defender still has to make the tackle.

It is critical that the quarterback is aware that he must go through every progression, and not have any preconceived notions. He needs to find the open receiver. Philosophically, most teams have a high percentage of pass calls in this situation.

All factors considered, the quarterback should have an option play ready to use in this down and distance. As such, teams need to run the ball often enough to keep the defense honest. The quarterback has to be aware that if it looks like an option check or a run check against a particular look by the defense will work he should let it rip. On the other hand, if it doesn't work, just as long as the offense finished the play with the ball, it's acceptable good.

Another huge coaching point for the championship quarterback is that punting the football is not necessarily a bad thing for the offense. It's OK to punt. Furthermore, showing an option or a run or two in this particular down-and-distance situation can be a great investment for the rest of the game.

The third-and-four to -six situation is one in which the percentages start going down with regard to conversion rates for the offense. A team that converts more than 60 percent on this down-and-distance situation is really rolling. It should also be noted that third-and-medium is a down-and-distance situation that if the offense is playing well, it will have more of these situations than any other third down situation in the game. As a rule, if the offense is playing well, there will be approximately eight of these situations in the game. The goal of the offense should be to convert at least five of them. Most importantly, they should try to convert the last one, the one that could occur with the game on the line.

Third-and-seven to -eight is more of an intermediate down-and-distance situation. This down-and-distance scenario is one on which some defensive coordinators will start to back off a little bit, while others will really bring the heat.

The quarterback should be taught that whatever route combination he calls, the ball doesn't have to go to the deepest progression. While some deeper routes may start to get called in this situation, the quarterback must learn to trust the call and trust his reads. It's not acceptable for him to force the football into coverage. Likewise, it certainly is not OK to start throwing bombs because of the down and distance. As discussed previously, because the conversion percentages go down in this situation, the quarterback must understand that he needs to take care of the football, keep the offense in relatively good situations, don't be afraid to check to an option or a screen, and once again, it's perfectly OK to punt.

Third-and-9 to -11 is a scenario in which a lot of defensive coordinators demonstrate their philosophy concerning longer down-and-distance situations. This situation is one in which a two-deep man under will show up, as well as Tampa 2. Whatever the philosophy of the defensive coordinator, the coverage will really start to show itself on film.

This down-and-distance situation is one in which some defenses really like to pour the coals to the offenses and back them up even further. It's also a down-and-distance situation on which the defense will rush three defenders and drop eight. Whatever the fronts and coverages are, after proper film study and adequate practice time, the quarterback should be aware of the fact that he is armed with a sufficient number of good calls. He should know that he doesn't have to throw the ball a mile down the field to get a first down. He should realize that there have been many occasions on which a check-down has been thrown, which gained a first down.

The quarterback should not force his passes. If he sees a particular defensive look, this may be a good time to call a run or a screen. Once again, the quarterback needs to know that it's acceptable to punt the football.

If the offense is playing really well, there won't be too many of these situations in the game. On the other hand, if the offense is playing poorly, there will be way too many. In either scenario, the quarterback must play the play, not force the ball, and make sure that the offense retains possession of it after the down is over.

Third-and-12-plus is a down on which many offenses simply give up. On numerous occasions, offensive coordinators just call a safe run and start yelling for the punt team. On the other hand, times will occur in this situation where a first down could be gained if the offensive staff and the quarterback have spent enough time watching film.

In this situation, defenses will often play a base front and a conservative coverage, a scenario that presents an opportunity to hit a play for a first down. The quarterback should be aware of the fact that he will have two to three calls at his disposal in this situation. He should understand the odds of each play being successful. Furthermore, he should also understand that no matter what happens, he must not force the football.

On a number of occasions, the quarterback can gain a first down simply going through his pass progressions, and not forcing balls deep. Hypothetically, the quarterback could also be facing a corner who doesn't play the deep ball well and can be beaten. Furthermore, that corner could panic and interfere with the receiver, when the ball goes up. As a rule, if the defensive back could catch the ball very well, he would probably be a receiver.

The quarterback should be aware that when this call comes in the game, he needs to get the ball up and out and give his receiver a chance to catch it. Given the circumstances, he should feel pretty good about his chances against such a corner. Either the receiver will catch the ball for a first down or he will get interfered with by the corner, since the corner has a history of not playing the ball well in the air. If by some chance, the defensive back catches the ball for an interception, the quarterback should view the errant throw like a punt.

If the quarterback has a working understanding of all the third down situations, as well as the underlying philosophy behind the calls he makes, he will have an enhanced chance to be successful. He must also realize the importance of not forcing the ball deep, just because of the situation he's facing. Furthermore, the quarterback must be aware of the need for him to go through each progression, and if the throw isn't there, to not take a sack, throw the ball away, and punt the football. The quarterback must be conscious of the fact that if his conversion rate is around 45 percent on all of his third downs, he is doing relatively well.

❑ Red zone. The red zone could be called the "must" zone for the offense and the quarterback. There are several musts that must happen when the offense gets to that particular area of the field. First, the quarterback must take care of the football at all costs, which means no turnovers.

In fact, the quarterback has to take the utmost care of the football at all times. For example, he must ensure that every handoff is made and secured properly. He also has to clearly see the receiver to whom he is throwing. When in doubt of whether a risk of the pass being intercepted exists, he needs to throw the football away. In that regard, there can never be any throws that are forced into coverage. Turnovers in the red zone will get a team beat.

The percentage that teams score when they reach the red zone is obviously much higher than otherwise, because the offense is closer to the goal line. As such, every possession is precious, and every trip to the red zone is valued. The quarterback has to understand that points must be gained on every trip to the red zone. The fact that taking care of the football must happen every trip to the red zone has to be drilled into his brain.

Another must for the quarterback is he must not take a sack in the red zone—ever. Sacks that are taken in the red zone usually put the offense behind the sticks, if the sack is taken on first or second down. This scenario can put too much pressure on the offense to execute a third-down-and-longer yardage call. If the sack is taken on third down, it may not only cost the offense a touchdown, on occasion, it may also take the offense out of field goal range.

Every time we practice in the red zone, whether it's a pass-skeleton session or a team session, I remind the quarterback to take care of the football and that he cannot take a sack. This point needs to be made on virtually every play, especially with a young quarterback. He must understand how critical it is to come out of the red zone with points.

Ideally, if the offense is a championship-caliber offense, it should score points upwards of 90 percent of the time in the red zone. This precept does not necessarily mean touchdowns, but it does mean points. As noted previously, it must be inculcated into the quarterback's brain that sacks and turnovers will not and cannot be tolerated. The importance of these coaching directives cannot be overstated. Virtually every trip to the red zone needs to result in points for the offense. Obviously, touchdowns are what the offense wants.

A good offense in the red zone can be an effective offense in the red zone if it can run the football effectively. If that is the case, then the offense needs to be a good naked team. Those two factors go hand in hand. One lives off of the other. Finally, an effective three-step passing game in the red zone helps to tie everything together. If an offense can accomplish those three elements, it has an excellent opportunity to be an excellent red zone offense.

Another factor that is often overlooked is the value of using cadence in the red zone. As a rule, defensive coordinators like to blitz in this particular area of the field because they know that if they can make a negative-yardage play or sack the quarterback, the offense can be taken out of field goal range. As such, if the quarterback uses a freeze-type cadence to force the defense to show its hand, the quarterback can often check his unit into a better play, one that will help undermine the defensive pressure that he just realized was coming, by holding the cadence.

The quarterback is the player who makes it all go. If his coach has done a good enough job of making him understand the "musts" of playing his position, he will have an enhanced chance to put the ball in the end zone when his team reaches the red zone.

❏ Goal line. The goal line is the most enjoyable situation in football. It is a gut check. While the offense has the advantage, to a degree, because of where the ball is, many times, it gets down to which team wants it the most. In fact, a number of championships have been won and lost on the goal line. When the ball is on the goal line, a coach can find out who his champions are. Put a ball down on the three-yard line, and it is attitude time.

A variety of different philosophies exist that offensive coaches have when their team is on the goal line. Some like to spread everything out, in an attempt to create some space and running lanes. Others like to bring heavier personnel in and try to pound the ball in for the score. Still others stay with their field offensive philosophy, and do what they do, so to speak.

Defensively, some defensive coordinators like to play man-to-man coverage exclusively down that low. A smaller percentage likes to zone everything off against a spread look by the offense. Whatever the philosophy, the situation is straightforward. The offense has to score, and the defense has to get a stop.

The quarterback must be aware of the fact that reading this area of the field must result in a touchdown. In other words, ensuring the security of every handoff, and executing the give, keep, or pitch on an option play, as well as taking care of the football and not forcing a throw, if it's not there.

The quarterback must display a gritty attitude and demeanor the opponent's goal line. As such, the quarterback must will the ball into the end zone. In that regard, he must be aware of the fact from how he's been coached that somehow, someway, the offensive unit needs to and will score a touchdown. For example, the quarterback must know what his coach's philosophy is when the ball gets to the three-yard line. In turn, the quarterback should realize that a pass will be called on at least one of the four downs. In that regard, on one hand, he needs to take great care of the football. On the other hand, he must be aware of the fact that he may have to make a tight throw in a tight spot.

Regardless of the mentality of the coaching staff, the quarterback is an extension of that philosophy. He must know that his team must score a touchdown when it reaches the goal line. Championships are won and lost on the goal line. If he is going to be a championship quarterback, the ball needs to be put over the goal line.

❏ Four-minute. Four-minute offense usually entails a scenario in which the offense has the ball, with a lead, and needs to get first downs in order to run the clock out and win the game. It encompasses a situation in which the defense needs a stop to get the ball back to their offense, in order for it to have a chance to win the game. As such, four-minute offense needs to be practiced by both sides of the ball. Typically, in its four-minute offense, the offense will try and run the football, and will only throw if it is necessary.

The main objective of the four-minute offense is to take time off of the clock and make first downs. Accordingly, it is extremely important for the quarterback to understand that the ball should be snapped with only approximately two seconds left on the 25-second clock. Furthermore, it is also important to note that when his team is in a four-minute mode, every player who touches the ball should make every attempt to stay inbounds to keep the clock running. It is also important to coach every player, who touches the ball, to get up slowly. Every effort should also be undertaken to make the official come and get the ball from whoever has touched the ball.

In the four-minute offense, the quarterback has to be aware of a number of factors. For example, there can be no penalties in this situation. Furthermore, stunts, blitzes, and all kinds of pressure from the defense should be anticipated. In addition, every player on the field should expect a desperate effort from the defense, an undertaking that may include the defense trying to strip the ball on every play.

To this point, much of this entire book has discussed the fact that a championship quarterback has the ability to execute a championship passing attack. If that is the case, then, philosophically, the coach should not be hesitant to call passes in a situation involving the four-minute offense. If the coach has confidence in his quarterback, passing in this situation can be a good thing.

Obviously, every pass needs to be completed because the clock stops, which is contrary to the underlying premise of the four-minute offense. While incomplete passes aren't good in this situation, completed passes can be invaluable, especially on first down. A completed pass generally puts the offense in favorable down-and-distance situations, as well as lets the defense know that they aren't facing a one-dimensional attack. Timeouts, if the defense has them, start to get burned. Furthermore, it is much more difficult to defend a multidimensional attack.

Four-minute offense is another test of wills between the offense and the defense. The quarterback must be aware of several factors. For example, he must know how many timeouts the defense has at any given point. He also needs to realize that there is no way he can allow a turnover to happen. Furthermore, he must understand that when a pass play is called, he should execute the play with the same swagger and confidence that he has displayed throughout the day.

The quarterback must also know that forcing the football in the four-minute offense can get his team beat. If the throw isn't there, he should simply try and get back to the line of scrimmage, if at all possible, as opposed to throwing the ball away, which will stop the clock.

The four-minute offense is really the only situation in which the throw-away isn't the right thing to do, because of what the offense is trying to do, which is to run the clock out. If it's third down, and the throw is not there, the quarterback should try and get back to the line of scrimmage by running. If that is not possible, he should simply throw the ball away, and then have his team punt and play defense. As such, it is imperative that the quarterback always understands that the name of the game is always to give his team a chance to win.

Because the defense is pretty close to being in a desperate situation when facing the four-minute offense, this set of circumstances is another great time to teach the quarterback to change the cadence on any third down-and-short call. Going on two or some type of hard count puts the defensive unit in this situation where it is more likely to jump offsides. Jumping offsides obviously creates a cheap first down for the offense. On many occasions, it also completely demoralizes a defense because of the situation they are in.

Changing his cadence in this situation can be a good thing for the quarterback. Not only can it help him get a cheap first down, it can also help him to hold the count on third down to see what he is getting defensively. Then, he can audible to a play that offers a better chance for success, because the defense has shown their hand. There isn't a better feeling than having the ball in a four-minute situation and then making first downs to end the game. The ability to execute in this situation provides some of the more gratifying times for the quarterback and his coach.

❏ Two-minute. Two-minute offense must be practiced weekly during the season. In fact, some of the best two-minute offenses actually work the drill more than once a week. Ideally, the first team offense needs to be put in two different situations from a time and a timeout standpoint each week during the season.

As such, the quarterback needs to be aware of the fact if the situation dictates that a touchdown or field goal is needed to tie or win the game, all four downs will be used in the drive. Furthermore, he needs to also understand that as a rule, his unit only needs one completion out of the four downs to get a first down. This situation is where the championship quarterback earns his stripes.

Every player on the offense, in fact, every athlete on the entire team, is looking to the quarterback to display poise, leadership, and toughness, as well as find a way to win, by getting the necessary points that are needed. The quarterback needs to be calm, cool, and collected, and do his job to the best of his ability. If a touchdown or field goal is needed, he will use all four downs, if necessary.

The quarterback also needs to understand that time is more important than the down. Every person on offense who touches the ball should be aware of the fact that they should get what they can on the play, and then get out of bounds, if at all possible. Anyone who touches the ball should know that if they get to the numbers of the field, they should work to get out of bounds.

As noted in previous scenarios, the quarterback must be aware that since time is more important than the down, he should throw the ball away and not take the sack. The quarterback should understand that taking a sack in a two-minute situation is just as bad or worse than taking a sack in the red zone. The quarterback also needs to know to take what the defense is giving him. As a rule, this factor should already be ingrained in him. On the other hand, it should be reinforced to him to not be greedy and dump the ball down, if that is what the defense is giving.

The quarterback should be trained to be sensitive to the time on the game clock. For example, if his team huddles, the only time that his unit will huddle in a two-minute drill is when the ball is dead, e.g., there has been an incomplete pass, or a timeout has been taken. Furthermore, the quarterback should be aware of the fact that after an offensive penalty, the clock will start as soon as the ball has been spotted.

In order to save a timeout there is a play that is universal to two-minute football— the "clock" play. On this play, the quarterback spikes the ball for an incomplete pass that stops the clock. The mechanics of this play are simple. Every player must sprint back to the line of scrimmage after the previous play and line up on the line of scrimmage. The players don't have to be in a stance of any kind. The quarterback knows that once everyone is set for a count, he then gives the command to the center to snap the ball. This command is a first sound call, obviously to get the ball snapped as soon as possible. It is very important that the quarterback hustle to the line of scrimmage and get under center quickly. Subsequently, as soon as everyone is set for a count, the ball is snapped.

A major coaching point, one that is often overlooked, is that it's very important for the quarterback to be acutely aware, during the two-minute drill, of when the official will be starting the clock. Unfortunately, quarterbacks at every competitive level often waste valuable time just standing on the field after the previous play has unfolded, just watching as valuable seconds tick off of the clock. This scenario involves hidden time that many coaches don't coach. If a two-minute drive, for example, goes for six or eight plays, and the quarterback lets two seconds go off the clock before snapping the ball each play, that is a waste of upwards of 15 to 16 seconds. That is a huge amount of time and can cost a team the game. Such an occurrence is the result of poor coaching, as well as poor quarterback play. The point to remember is that as soon as the official waves his arm to start the clock, the ball should be snapped.

The best two-minute offenses operate with extreme confidence. Nothing fancy has to be done. The quarterback should exude extreme confidence, not only as a by-product of his preparation for the moment, but also his understanding that if everyone on his unit just does his job, the chances for success are great. All factors considered, the championship quarterback realizes that the defense has way more pressure on it, because of the great challenge it faces with regard to stopping an offense that is operating at a very high level and defending a quarterback who won't be denied.

❏ Last play of the game. The last play of the game or last plays of the game are typically broken down into three scenarios. First, when the offense has to score a touchdown to win and it is backed up too far to get the ball close to the end zone on a Hail Mary-type pass. The second scenario entails the offense being close enough to midfield to at least attempt such a throw. The third scenario involves a situation in which the offense has the ball around the 30-yard line or closer and has to make an attempt at the end zone. In all three of these scenarios, the clock is about to expire, and there isn't time or timeouts left to either huddle or for the coaching staff to think of something to call.

When the ball is too far to make an attempt at a Hail Mary pass to the end zone, there are different thoughts by coaching staffs with regard to what is the best way to get the ball to the end zone. The possibilities are endless. For most coaches, however, it seems that the situation will usually involve a pass down the field and then have the player who caught the ball toss the ball backwards to a teammate, who then looks to do the same. The process subsequently continues all the way down the field.

This is not a play that should just be pulled out of the hat. Rather, it should be practiced at least once a week. In this scenario, the quarterback has to know the situation and has to be able to communicate the play to his teammates, without any call coming from the side line. As such, the quarterback needs to be aware of how much time is on the clock and where the ball is located on the field. He then automatically makes the call at the line.

In reality, a number of different plays could be employed as the call on the last play of the game. Whatever the staff ultimately decides to call, however, must be communicated to the quarterback. As such, it must be practiced each week. Because this scenario can and will come up during the course of a season, it must be understood by the quarterback. His understanding of the situation can make between running a play and giving his team a chance to win, or not even getting any sort of organized play off.

The third scenario is one of the most discussed situations by coaches across the country, because it really has no right answer. The offense is too close to lob up a Hail Mary, given that the ball could be anywhere from the 30-yard line to the two-yard line. What is the call? As such, coaches hold a variety of different philosophies regarding what to do that are essentially irrelevant for the quarterback. He must be fully aware of the situation he is in and must get the right call in to his teammates.

As discussed previously, he will give his team an opportunity to win the game if he knows and understands what the call is. On the other hand, if the quarterback is unaware of the timeout situation or how much time is on the game clock, it could cost his team a last play or a shot at the end zone. This scenario is just one more example of situational football and one more example of it being imperative that the quarterback is completely schooled on what he should do in each and every set of circumstances.

❏ Overtime. Playing in overtime is another battle of wills between teams. Conceptually, it is much like red zone offense for the quarterback, except that both teams get an opportunity to score. If the quarterback's offense gets the ball first in the overtime period, he needs to know that even though everyone wants a touchdown, kicking a field goal is OK.

The same key principles apply in overtime as they do in normal red zone offense. Ball security is a must. The offense can't have penalties because that can result in third down-and-long situations, making it hard to convert and possibly even taking the offense out of field goal range. The quarterback has to understand that he cannot take a sack. Sacks are worse than penalties, because not only has the offense lost yardage, on numerous occasions, it also gives the defense a substantial boost in momentum. Furthermore, the quarterback needs to realize that if he gets in trouble, he has to throw the ball away, given that points are at a premium.

As a rule, most teams that win the toss for overtime choose to play defense first, so that their offense will know if it needs to kick a field goal or score a touchdown. Accordingly, the quarterback has to be aware of the fact that he can't force the football. A turnover in overtime can pretty much guarantee defeat for his team.

The offensive strategy in overtime is similar to the strategy employed in the red zone, because of the area of the field in which the ball is placed initially, and because most defenses know that they need to create lost-yardage plays in order to take the offense out of scoring range. Similar to the red zone, the quarterback can expect to encounter stunts, blitzes, and pressures in this situation.

Somewhat surprisingly, a few offensive coordinators exist who like to use overtime as a time to show something different offensively than what they have utilized during the course of the game. On occasion, even a trick play that hasn't been used during the game, one that can be executed on a short field, will be tried. Whatever play is called, however, the quarterback must realize that his offensive unit can't afford to have penalties or turnovers. The offense has to take great care of the football. Furthermore, the quarterback has to be aware of the fact that not only can he not take a sack, but throwing the football away is a must because forcing a throw into coverage can result in an interception, which pretty much ends the game.

All factors considered, the quarterback sometimes has to be relatively resilient in overtime, because each team gets a turn to score. On occasion, multiple overtimes sometimes occur. In fact, the greatest number of overtimes in NCAA history is seven. As such, the quarterback can't get on the roller coaster of emotions during overtime. The quarterback must stay locked in, in the moment, and focus on the next play. This scenario is one in which all the traits covered in this book come into play.

The quarterback must display great poise during overtime. The championship quarterback will help guide his teammates though the range of emotions that occur during either single or multiple overtime games. His poise, toughness, and determination will tend to rub off on his teammates as they collectively find a way to win the game together.

CHAPTER 11
Drills for Problem Throwers

There are very few programs in the country that don't have a quarterback or quarterbacks who need help mechanically. From the NFL, all the way down to Pop Warner football, there are quarterbacks who are struggling and need help with one mechanical-related issue or another. The problem can be seen in the most high profile games in the country on national television, as well as every time a game film is turned on in a coach's office.

For the most part, quarterbacks want to be coached. For the most part, they also want to get better. Championship quarterbacks want to be great. Part of being great is having sound mechanics—better yet, consistently sound mechanics.

A substantial number of quarterbacks exist who need to be coached and want to be coached, but continue to struggle week after week, season after season. Yet, when I go to coaching clinics or read many of the publications that are available, all I ever hear quarterback coaches and offensive coordinators talk about is scheme. Everyone wants to talk about the latest and greatest pass route or the latest and greatest way to block a run play. Schemes are overrated. People aren't. Very rarely, do quarterback coaches talk about how to coach the position or, more importantly, how to coach the mechanics of the position.

For years, the NFL never had quarterback coaches. During that period, the offensive coordinator met with the quarterbacks, and all the quarterback got was X's and O's in the meeting room. Every time the next quarterback "guru" emerges on any level of football, the topic is most always schematic. The issue of coaching some quarterback mechanics, however, needs to be addressed.

Before this chapter presents drills for the problem thrower, it can be helpful to review what the proper mechanics of throwing the football should look like. The following eight elements constitute the basic fundamental mechanics essential in throwing the football:

- Have a wide base.
- Have weight back (at a 75 percent to 25 percent distribution, i.e., 75 percent of the weight should shift back).
- Take a short step.
- Step slightly to the left of the target.
- Keep the elbow of the throwing arm parallel to the ground or higher.
- Have a "Z" in the knee.
- Keep the head still.
- Follow through.

Much like the golfer who's taking swing lessons and 100 different things to think about from a golf pro, while the golfer is over the ball, what usually happens? I know what happens to me. I get so caught up in trying to do all 100 things that I still can't hit the ball.

In my opinion, the coach's focus with the quarterback should be on the aforementioned eight basic fundamentals, not only because they are doable, but also because they are vitally important in the mechanics of the throw. Are there other important points in how to throw the football? Absolutely. In my opinion, however, once these eight points are mastered, some of the other points easily follow suit.

Power and accuracy come from the lower body. It doesn't matter what sport it is, the ability of the individual to shift his weight and transfer power from his lower body is the key component in generating maximum power and weight shift. As such, if these eight coaching points are mastered, it will lead to the quarterback being more powerful, accurate, and consistent.

A list of five of the most often seen flaws that quarterbacks have all over the country and on every competitive level include the following:

- Low release point
- Long, slow loopy release
- Overstriding
- Doesn't fully get open to the target
- Locks lead leg

❏ Low release point. The first common mistake is a quarterback who has a low release point, e.g., a low elbow. The problem with quarterbacks who have a low release point is they tend to be less accurate than the quarterbacks who have a release point with their elbow parallel to the ground or higher.

Besides Kenny Stabler and Bernie Kosar in the old days and possibly Philip Rivers who is currently active in the NFL, it's hard to name a prolific passing quarterback with a low release point, who is extremely accurate. It's much like individuals who like to throw darts in the pub. They drop their elbow and aim at the target.

When throwing a football, when the quarterback drops his elbow, there also tends to be some aiming involved. Furthermore, when a quarterback tries to aim the ball, errant passes are soon to follow. When a quarterback drops his elbow, the ball tends to sail. The other major problem with quarterbacks who have a low-release point is that they get many more balls batted down at the line of scrimmage than quarterbacks who have a higher release point.

A great drill for the quarterback who drops his elbow is an easy drill to set up. As such, if the quarterback will take the coaching, he will be able raise his release point and be able to "get on top of his ball" on his release. The first step in the drill is to get your quarterback to stand on a yard line, with a wide base, his weight back, and his lead shoulder on his target. Then, have a receiver stand 10 yards away from the quarterback, giving him a target right in front of his face. Next, have whoever else is available stand in between the quarterback and receiver, five yards in between the two. It could be an extra quarterback or a manager. If necessary, the quarterback coach could assume that position, as well. Next, have the extra individuals put their hands up and extend their arms as high as they can.

Figure 11-1. High elbow drill

The first coaching point for the quarterback should be to push the ball back and up, an action that will really raise his elbow higher than he is used to raising it.

Figure 11-2. The first coaching point for the quarterback in the high elbow drill should be to push the ball back and up.

The second coaching point should be to have the quarterback throw the ball with maximum arm speed. It should feel to him like he is trying to rip a 15-yard dig route on a line. This scenario is exactly like a pitcher who throws a change-up and doesn't change his arm speed or delivery. He just changes the location of where he puts the ball in his hand. Instead of gripping the ball with his fingers, he puts the ball back in the palm of his hand.

At first, the quarterback will try to aim the ball over the outstretched hands of the defenders by not really whipping his arm through, an action that is sometimes referred to as "pulling the window shade down." Make him rip that "window shade" down. By exerting maximum arm speed, it will pull his ball down to where the receiver can catch the ball at the target.

At first, the ball will sail, because the quarterback won't use his normal arm speed. The next thing that typically occurs is that he will drop his elbow back to his comfort zone, and the ball will never get over the arms of the defenders. Make the quarterback with a low-release point warm up every day doing this drill. His first 25 throws should all start with this drill.

If the quarterback really wants to change and will work hard at it all winter or all summer, this drill will get his elbow up, which will enable him to get on top of his ball. His coach will know that his quarterback has really improved, when he can move him two to eight yards away from the receiver, and he can still get his ball up and out and over the outstretched arms of the defenders.

❏ Long, slow, loopy release. The next problem that quarterbacks have is a long, slow, loopy release. This is a release that starts out in the middle of the quarterback's body and then loops down around his hip and goes back for days, before he finally throws the football. The primary problem with this type of release is that it is so long and loopy, too much room for error exists in this motion. Another problem with this type of release is that it is very slow.

One drill that will help take the loop out of the quarterback's release is to stand him against a wall. Everything should touch the wall. His butt, his heels, his shoulders, and the back tip of the ball should all be in contact with the wall. His elbow should be up at the proper release point.

Figure 11-3. Wall drill

To conduct the drill, have the quarterback throw to a buddy, who is standing 10 yards away. Because the quarterback has no momentum with the long release, he is stripped of all his power. In fact, he will struggle getting the ball the full 10 yards. Eventually, as he continues to work, he will become more comfortable, and his arm will actually get stronger. At some point, he will be able to back his buddy up farther and farther away.

This drill shortens the quarterback's motion and teaches him to just get the ball back, as opposed to dropping down and then taking it back. If the quarterback will work on this drill every day, over the course of the winter months or summer months, his loop will be eliminated. He should start every warm-up session with 25 of these throws, before he ever throws another ball. As noted, if the quarterback will work with determined effort and put the work in with this drill, his big circular release will disappear.

❑ Overstriding. The next major problem that can be seen by quarterback coaches everywhere is the quarterback who overstrides. A quarterback can overstride either when he is at the top of his drop or when he takes a hitch or shuffle step, when he's starting to throw. In fact, quarterbacks overstride so bad on occasion that they will actually click their heels when they stride to throw the football.

When a quarterback overstrides, he becomes less accurate. When he overstrides, his ball will tend to sail or go in the dirt. At the proper release point, the quarterback should be able to drive a rod from the palm of his hand, through the front of his chest, through his front kneecap, and down through the bottom of the ball of his lead foot. A quarterback who overstrides can't do that. That same rod would go down his back in some cases. His arm would never catch up with his body, which is what makes his ball sail or go in the dirt.

A simple, but very effective, drill for the overstrider is to get a concrete block and put it four to six inches away from the quarterback to simulate a short step. At that point, have the quarterback assume a wide base, with his weight back, and then step and throw to a receiver who initially is in a position 10 yards away. At first, the quarterback's lead foot will bang the concrete block over and over. As he warms up, make this drill be the first thing he does. Eventually, he will not need the concrete block to help his muscle memory of taking a short step. The quarterback can move from right to left and left to right. As long as he gets in position to have that concrete block right in front of him, his overstriding will start to disappear.

Figure 11-4. Concrete block drill

❏ Doesn't fully get open to the target. A major problem with some quarterbacks is they don't properly step with their lead foot to get fully open to their target, which makes a full weight shift impossible. The quarterback, if he is right-handed, should step slightly to the left of his target. It should actually be about two inches to the left of his target. Even stepping directly at his target, a line could be drawn from his belly button that would point to about two on the face of a clock, which means that his hips aren't fully open, making a full weight shift impossible. The quarterback will actually be throwing against his body, which puts more stress on his shoulder and elbow.

If the quarterback steps slightly to the left of his target, that same line could be drawn from his belly button to his target, and it would be directly at the target. His hips are fully open, which makes a full weight shift possible. As a consequence, he will be able to generate more power. This positioning also results in less stress on his shoulder and elbow, which, in turn, leads to quarterbacks not missing valuable practice time with sore arms.

I like the following drill for the quarterback who doesn't fully get open to his target. Place a brick right at the target and make the quarterback simply step to the left of the brick. If done properly, the quarterback will step to the left of the brick, which will put him about two inches past his target. Initially, the quarterback will step either directly on the brick or on the side of the brick. Eventually, he will be able to consistently step past the brick, which will put his lead foot and hips in proper alignment for the desired weight shift. As with the other drills in this chapter have the quarterback warm up every day doing this drill. If the quarterback is faithful in his efforts with this drill, the problem will disappear.

Figure 11-5. Brick drill

❏ Locks lead leg. The final problem that is covered in this chapter is the quarterback who locks his lead leg when he's throwing. It happens far too often. In fact, some quarterbacks lock their lead leg so badly it looks like they may hyperextend their knee. These quarterbacks are losing major power on both their intermediate throws and deep balls, because the weight shift that started so well comes to a screeching halt when the quarterback is straight up and down. The quarterback who is in a straight-up-and-down position looks somewhat like the golfer who is trying to hit a knockdown nine iron in a golf tournament. His club has barely hit the ball, and his follow-through is stopped, which is what happens to this quarterback.

When the quarterback's lead leg locks, all power ceases. All of his weight shift is stopped. He will lose five to eight yards on a deep ball. Furthermore, a ball that should be ripped in there on a curl route doesn't have the juice on it like it should.

A great drill to help address this problem involves obtaining an angle board out of the training room or using a brick or concrete block. The drill also entails getting a 1x10 board and putting it on the brick or block to create an angle that is close to 45 degrees. Then have the quarterback step on this board when he's striding. What occurs by doing this drill over and over is that the quarterback starts to feel what it feels like to hit with a "Z" in his knee.

As with the other drills, have the quarterback start practice by warming up with this technique. Conversely, then put the board on the other side of the brick or block, and make him step on the board. As a result, he can feel what hitting with a "Z" in his knee does, as he experiences the full weight shift. He will feel his back leg coming off the ground, as 100 percent of his weight is shifted.

Figure 11-6. "Z" in the knee

Figure 11-7. Follow-through

All of the drills detailed in this chapter have been proven effective. These drills will work if the quarterback is coached properly, particularly if he really works on them. Over the course of my career, I've had quarterbacks, who have worked every day all summer long for 10 weeks on all of these problems, come to camp and not look like the same individual, who, at one time of another had these flaws. It's a want-to issue. If it's important enough for the quarterback to put the work in, every single one of the problems can be eliminated.

CHAPTER 12
Individual Drills, Group Drills, and Team Drills

The purpose of drills is to make the individual better by simulating situations that occur during the course of a particular play that help determine the outcome of that play, as well as, ultimately, the game. Drills should be as realistic as possible from a mental and physical standpoint. Individual drills for the quarterback should help put the athlete in the best possible position to have success by simulating realistic situations that occur and by incorporating the necessary repetitions that reinforce great mechanics that will allow for success.

Inexplicably, there are a number of highly paid quarterback "gurus" working with athletes, who have their quarterbacks perform many highly orchestrated and elaborate drills that don't truly simulate what quarterbacks really do in the passing game. Running over bags and running from one cone to the next don't simulate what it's like either in the pocket or when trying to move within or outside the pocket. If the quarterback has to pick his feet up to step over bodies in and around the pocket, the coach either needs to change protectors or change protections.

Running from one cone to the next doesn't simulate the quarterback's movement in and around the pocket either. Quarterbacks move to open areas to help them see and help them secure a place to try and accurately throw the football, not move to predetermined areas marked by objects.

Except for a couple of quarterbacks who play in the best league in the world, the NFL, 99 percent of quarterbacks need routine, rhythm, and fundamentals to allow themselves the chance to complete passes consistently. The other factor that quarterbacks need is tools to help them when their routine and rhythm is disrupted by oncoming rushers and defenders.

Previous chapters have addressed the necessary mechanics for throwing the ball with power, accuracy, and consistency. Drills that help enhance those mechanics have been covered. This chapter presents drills (individual, group, and team) that are designed to help facilitate the aforementioned mechanics, as well as help develop a championship quarterback. Similar to the drills in Chapter 11, these drills also need to be done every practice day of the football season.

❏ Individual drills. The number one drill for giving a quarterback the best chance to successfully throw the football is simply to practice dropping. As such, three-step, five-step, and play-action pass drops should be done every day.

The purpose of this drill is three-fold. First, it helps the quarterback reach his proper depth within the concept. Second, it helps the quarterback understand to always hit with a wide base, with his weight back. Always hitting with a wide base and his weight back allows the proper mechanics of the throw to occur and aids in his routine and rhythm. Third, working on all the various drops every day and by giving the quarterback a play before each rep, helps with the internal clock in the quarterback's head with the individualized timing aspects of each concept, as well as with any coverage or blitz adjustment that goes with a particular play.

In reality, pass drop drills aren't sexy. They won't win an award for the coach with the prettiest drills. They will, however, give the quarterback his best chance to be successful, while throwing in the pocket in rhythm.

The best way to teach the proper way to drop is to have the quarterback straddle a line in a proper stance. Whether the quarterback is under center or in the gun, a proper stance starts it all. Straddling a line gives the quarterback a great reference point for his first step. His first step should come straight back and hit on the line.

One of the worst things a quarterback can do on his first step is to "step in the bucket." Stepping in the bucket is a situation in which the quarterback steps past six on the clock. If the quarterback steps in the bucket, it closes his hips more than they should, which makes it harder to get his hips properly open, especially when he's throwing to his left.

If the quarterback is taking a three-step drop from under center and is a right-handed quarterback, he should mentally put his weight on the ball of his left foot. He should drive off that left foot and reach for depth. It should hit on the line that is being straddled. His second step should be his control step or brake step. This step is shorter and more controlled. It will aid in stopping his momentum and help him come to a firm and complete stop on his third step. His shoulders, on the second step, should be perpendicular to the line of scrimmage. On his third step, he should always hit with a wide base and his weight back. An ideal depth from the line of scrimmage is four to four and a half yards.

When throwing a three-step drop from under center and throwing a predetermined route to his left, the quarterback should step at more of an angle to his right with his first step. As previously noted, the yard line is a good landmark for the quarterback to see if his first step is short of 6 o'clock and more at 4 o'clock on the face of a clock. Stepping like this aids the quarterback in being able to get his hips open when throwing to his left. His second and third steps should be on the same angle as his first. The quarterback's depth won't be quite as deep, but it will allow his hips to be more open to his target to his left, which will ultimately aid in a better weight shift and in making a more consistently accurate throw.

There are a couple of routes where the quarterback won't hit and throw, when he hits on his third step. A second window slant or an option route by a tight end requires the quarterback to "hit and sit." In other words, he should keep his weight on his back foot and allow the route a little more time to develop.

The quarterback is aligned at a five-yard depth in a three-step drop from the shotgun. His first step should be with his left foot for a right-handed quarterback. It should be a short punch step. This step will look the same as the quarterback's first step on a five-step drop from the gun. Having his first steps look the same on both a three-step drop and a five-step drop helps prevent defenders from being able to easily read a three-step drop and get a jump and drive on the route.

The quarterback's next step should be with his right foot. His right foot should be at 6 o'clock, which will allow him to sit down, with a wide base and his weight back. When the quarterback hits in this manner, he should be ready to deliver the football. As previously noted, there are a couple of routes, e.g., a second window slant or an option route by a tight end, on which he won't hit and throw. He should "hit and sit" with his weight on his back foot. This technique enables him to adjust on a three-step route that takes a fraction of a second longer to develop.

The various coaching points that have been raised in this book need to be emphasized on a regular basis. If his mechanics aren't worked on daily, the quarterback can easily develop bad habits and inconsistent drops. With regard to a quarterback's drops, it is essential to understand that the consistency of the drop is almost as important as the mechanics of the drop. It is that consistency that gives the quarterback a maximum comfort level that is crucial, before he delivers the football.

If 15 minutes are devoted to a quarterback's individual work time, a full 10 minutes of that allotment should be devoted to drops. Besides helping the quarterback develop a routine with the fundamentals and mechanics that are addressed, it aids in the rhythm of the passing game. Rhythm is a huge component of a championship passing attack.

All factors considered, more time should be devoted to the five-step drop mechanics than any other schematic drop if that is what the team's offense is predicated on. Obviously, if its offense is predicated on three-step or play-action, then those areas should be addressed more. For most offenses, three-step and play-action passes might account for 30 percent of the passing game. In other words, in those situations, the five-step passing game provides the bulk of the workload for the quarterback and the offense.

A five-step drop from under center should start out like a three-step drop from under center. The quarterback should straddle a line with a proper stance. His weight should mentally be put on the ball of his left foot if he is a right-handed quarterback. He should drive off with his left foot and gain maximum depth on his first step. His second step should be in line with his first step. His shoulders should be perpendicular to the line of scrimmage. His third step should be another depth step. His fourth step should be his brake step and his fifth step should put the quarterback down on terra firma, with a wide base and his weight back.

The quarterback's eyes should always be downfield. An easy way to make sure that his eyes are where they are supposed to be is for the coach to stand in front of the quarterback and flash a number with his fingers. Any number chosen, from one through five, is fine as long as the quarterback yells out and identifies the number of fingers that the coach held up.

Once it is established that the quarterback's eyes are where they are supposed to be, the coach can start incorporating plays to make the quarterback understand the proper progression for the play, based on coverage and/or blitz. The coach can initiate this drill progression by simply telling the quarterback what coverage he is working against. At that point, the quarterback can simply yell out what his progression is and then go to the next progression and the next, and so on.

When undertaking this exercise, it is extremely important that the quarterback's feet move in accordance with his next progression. If the first progression is over the ball, his base, shoulders, and eyes should be there as well. If his next progression moves to the curl area, his base, shoulders, and eyes should follow. Every time a quarterback is capable of getting his feet, shoulders, and eyes aligned with his target, his chances of success are enhanced.

A five-step drop from the gun should begin with a short punch step. The next step should be with the quarterback's right foot, if he is right-handed. Since the quarterback is already five yards deep, a big first step is really not required. The second step is the brake step, on which his shoulders should be perpendicular to the line of scrimmage. On his third step, the quarterback should be planted, with a wide base and his weight back.

An ideal depth is seven to seven and a half yards deep. It is important to note that a quarterback can get too deep in the gun by taking too deep of a first step or taking extra steps. The pocket is not built for a quarterback who is too deep in the pocket on a five-step drop from the gun. For the quarterback who gets eight and a half and nine yards deep, the defensive end can end up being run right to the quarterback. Too many quarterbacks drop too deep and either have to shuffle up or end up taking a sack because of their misstepping.

Quarterbacks can never do too many of these drops for previously noted reasons. Although a quarterback will probably never be able to go an entire game being able to drop and throw on rhythm, ideally, he should be able to drop and throw on rhythm the majority of the time. This scenario is an opportunity, however, for the quarterback to enhance his ability to throw completions. The most effective way to achieve this objective is for the quarterback to be in position mechanically to make the best throw.

For the play-action teams, every play-action pass could involve a different run action. As such, it has its own eccentricity. Every one of them should be practiced with the same underlying premise as the three-step and the five-step drop mentality, which is to get in the best position possible with the lower body to make an accurate throw. In other words, the quarterback has to hit the ground as he stops to throw, after being on the move, with a wide base and his weight back.

At that point, the quarterback should take a short step, slightly to the left of the target. His elbow should be parallel to the ground or higher. His lead leg should hit with a "Z" in his knee to permit his weight to shift. His head should stay still through the throwing motion and follow-through should occur. These are the mechanics that should be closely watched for when the quarterback finishes his drop and actually simulates a throw.

Normally, after three drops to the right and the left for all three categories of throws, we finish every particular drop with a simulated throw on a route that was given to the quarterback before the play. On every progression, the quarterback should make sure that his feet, shoulders, and eyes are in the proper position and are doing what they should be doing. The quarterback should be told on what number progression to simulate the throw. The quarterbacks should look like synchronized swimmers in that they should all look the same with their mechanics. If someone looks differently, a reason exists for that.

The next progression in this series of drop drills can involve adding defenders, extra quarterbacks, managers, and coaches to the exercises, while the quarterback is going through his drops. This added feature can incorporate yet another challenge to the drill, when the quarterback isn't told what progression to work. For example, the defenders could be aligned in a coverage that could indicate to the quarterback how to progress on a particular pass play. In another hypothetical situation, the defenders could cover a route in a way that indicates to the quarterback to whom to throw the ball. The variety of defensive looks can be achieved with mixing up coverages, blitz looks, or just defenders moving toward a particular receiver.

Pretty much any variable the coach wants to throw in during a quarterback drop drill can be a good idea. This drill offers a great opportunity to work on routes that have hot throws to reinforce to the quarterback who his hot receiver is and the timing that is involved in getting the ball out. Coverage rotation with different routes is also a viable alternative.

It is important to be aware of the fact that a quarterback with great mechanics, who happens to throw the ball to a wrong receiver, has a better chance of completing a pass and moving the chains than does the quarterback, who is trying to throw the ball to the right receiver with lousy mechanics. For the quarterback coach who is interested in developing consistency with his quarterback, there is no drill or number of drills that can replace the quarterback who practices drops every practice day of the football season.

There probably have been very few games that a quarterback hasn't had to make a throw under duress. In fact, several times during the course of a game, the quarterback might have to move off of his perfect spot to see the field clearly. Furthermore, the quarterback may not always be in the perfect position with his feet or even his release point. These examples help illustrate why the quarterback should work on his movement within the pocket.

When the quarterback has to move in the pocket, he should adhere to the following fundamental footwork mechanics:

• Keep a wide base.
• Keep his feet low to the ground; shuffle, if possible.
• Push off with his back foot.

When the quarterback is moved off his spot by the rush, it is very important for him to work hard at keeping a wide base. This base helps ensure that he doesn't overstride. As a result, he will be more likely to make an accurate throw. Are there going to be times when the quarterback can't keep his wide base, because of duress or a lack of space? Of course. On the other hand, for the same reason that the quarterback strives to have a wide base in every other passing situation, he should work to keep his base wide and move with shuffle steps or "baby shuffles," if at all possible.

Another factor that is essential to having good footwork mechanics in the pocket is that the quarterback's feet need to stay as low to the ground as possible. Ideally, his feet would never come more than two inches off the ground. The quarterback should strive to keep as many cleats in the ground as he can. Quarterbacks who pick their feet up high lose valuable milliseconds when trying to move. For this reason alone, quarterbacks, who practice running and stepping over dummies, are wasting their time. They are practicing something that shouldn't happen in the game and practicing something that is not a proper fundamental of movement. If the quarterback naturally has live feet, and he moves like a sewing machine in the pocket, that's OK as long as he is not on his toes. Live feet are good in the pocket, but they certainly aren't a prerequisite for effective movement within the pocket.

It is important that the quarterback is aware of the fact that in order to keep his base to the best of his ability, he needs to push off with his back foot when he's moving. In other words, when it's time to execute a shuffle up in the pocket, the quarterback needs to push off with his back foot. The quarterback who attempts to initiate a shuffle off his front foot will find it difficult to generate any power. Such a scenario tends to make his back leg chase his front leg, which causes him to lose his base. If the quarterback has to step to his left or his right to be able to see or throw, the push-off needs to be done with his back foot, as well.

The movements of the quarterback in the pocket involve the following three elements:

- Move to throw in the pocket.
- Move to scramble to throw.
- Move to run.

The ability to move within the pocket to create space and to be able to see is crucial in the development of the quarterback. The number one factor a quarterback must do when he has to move off his spot is to never throw the ball to a receiver whom he doesn't clearly see. In reality, this mandate applies anytime a quarterback throws the football. It is a fact of life that quarterbacks who throw to targets that they can't clearly see are quarterbacks who are going to turn the ball over sooner or later. It is important when simulating a situation in which the quarterback has to move, that he still execute the proper fundamentals of the movement.

The first drill that should be performed is the "baby shuffle" drill. Not only is it relatively easy to do, but also of extreme value for the quarterback who needs to be able to execute under duress.

When conducting this drill, simply have the quarterback simulate where he is at the top of his drop on a yard line. His base should be wide, and his weight should be back. On command, have him start shuffling, attempting to get as many shuffles as possible in five yards. It is necessary to start out at five yards in order to emphasize how small his shuffle steps need to be. As such, he should strive to shuffle no more than two or three inches with each shuffle. More often than not, quarterbacks won't understand this directive, and will take way too long of a shuffle.

The primary reason for working on doing "baby shuffles" is to emphasize to the quarterback to not lose his base when he's moving. A quarterback who takes too long of a shuffle step is a quarterback who is going to lose his base. As a result, his feet will come too close together, which will result in him overstriding. The coach also should emphasize to the quarterback the need for him to keep his weight back to ensure that he has as much power that he can generate when it's time for him to throw. When the coach is comfortable with the quarterback's execution of the small shuffles that are an integral part of the exercise, the drill can be modified to be conducted in a 10-yard space. Extending the length of the drill can help create muscle memory for the quarterback at this distance.

A number of different ways exist to simulate movement within the pocket. It can be done with a defender running at the quarterback from one direction and having the quarterback simply slide either away from the pressure or up from the pressure, depending on the angle of the rush. Two or three rushers could be added to make the quarterback make a decision on an escape route, while still keeping his base and his eyes downfield.

It is important to note that the quarterback should not shuffle up farther than he has to. Doing so would bring him closer to the rush and make the throwing lanes tighter, because of the closer proximity of his subsequent location to the line of scrimmage. These movement drills are easy to do and can be incorporated during individual drills with the quarterbacks or even in drills in which the quarterbacks are throwing to receivers, backs, or tight ends, later in practice.

Doing these movement drills with the quarterbacks actually throwing to his teammates helps the quarterback practice making an accurate throw, when he's moved off his spot. When the quarterback is practicing throwing individual routes, it is a good idea to incorporate some type of movement for him every third or fourth throw. To a degree, this procedure would simulate what it might be like for him during the course of a ballgame.

During pass skeleton drills, it is a good idea to take the kickers, managers, and whoever else is available and have them stand on the line of scrimmage, with their hands up to help simulate bodies being at the line of scrimmage and to force the quarterback to have to move every so often. This technique simulates having the quarterback have to move within the pocket and find a throwing lane around the bodies in front of him. All factors considered, this exercise is about as realistic as the coach can make it, without it being a full-team passing drill.

When the quarterback can't shuffle up or slide within the pocket because there is too much inside pressure, occasions will occur when he will have to leave the pocket. As was discussed previously, it is always a viable idea for the quarterback to scramble to throw the football. Huge plays can sometimes result when the quarterback who scrambles has his eyes downfield.

When simulating a scramble situation, the coach can have two, perhaps even three, rushers come up the middle and force the quarterback to escape to his right or left. When conducting this drill, it is important to watch the quarterback's eyes to ensure when he makes his breaks, his eyes are downfield, looking for a receiver. After doing this drill a time or two, the coach could then add a receiver to the mix, and make the quarterback move and make an accurate throw on the run.

It is important to emphasize that when throwing the ball on the run, the quarterback should keep his chest up and get his lead shoulder back, so that he can run toward his target and "follow his ball." For a right-handed quarterback throwing to his left, the quarterback should literally rip his right shoulder back and out of the way, so that he can "follow his ball" after the throw. "Following the ball" helps ensure that the quarterback can still get on top of his ball, as well as help ensure that the ball won't be thrown in front of his receiver.

Some right-handed quarterbacks, who have to escape out of the pocket to their left, feel more comfortable actually turning their back to escape, as opposed to fronting out to escape. Not only can this technique add a little more depth to their escape route, it also can aid the quarterback, on occasion, in his efforts to pull away from an arm tackle.

The scramble drill that was discussed previously is an exercise that can be done every day during 7-on-7 sessions. In reality, it is yet another way to incorporate scrambling to throw into the quarterback's daily practice routine.

The third key area involved when the quarterback moves in the pocket is moving to run. On occasion, the defense has a twist stunt on or a nose guard in an odd front who gets washed out of his rush lane. As a result, the defense parts like the Red Sea. When this scenario occurs, the quarterback often just takes off. Even for the quarterback who moves and scrambles to throw, when the defense parts right in front of his face, it can become instinctive for him to run. If this scenario occurs, it is critical that the quarterback not only takes care of the football, he also needs to take care of himself.

A number of philosophies exist concerning whether the quarterback should slide or not when he is about to be tackled. Regardless of his coach's preference, the quarterback needs to be aware of the fact that unless he is fighting to get a first down or touchdown, he must not take a big hit, if at all possible. If a quarterback decides to slide, he should go feet first, which will prevent his head from being on the receiving end of forceful impact. While it is essential to teach a quarterback to move to scramble to throw, it is also important to remember that there have been many important games won by a quarterback, who takes off and keeps a drive alive, when he sees a huge hole in front of him. This capability can be an important part of the game. As such, it should receive attention both on the field and in the meeting room.

Throwing on the run should be practiced every day. As a rule, it normally doesn't take very long to do what needs to get done. The best and easiest way to practice throwing on the run is to position quarterbacks 20 yards apart on different yard lines and then have them run down their respective yard lines. Initially, they should go nice and slow, throwing to one another. The thrower should stay on the yard line and work on keeping his chest up and ripping his lead shoulder out of the way to allow him to be on top of the ball and to "follow his ball." The receiver should work to get a few steps in front of the quarterback who is throwing to him. After he catches the ball, he should then throttle down and let his teammate get a few steps in front of him, so that they can undertake the same procedure. Two times across the field and back, picking up speed with each time across the field, should be sufficient to get some good work in on throwing on the run. This exercise could be incorporated in the quarterback's warm-up, as well.

❏ Group drills. All factors considered, quarterbacks tend to be very popular at practice. Everyone wants a piece of the quarterback. The running backs want to be handed off to and thrown to. Tight ends want to be thrown to. Receivers are dying to be thrown to. Even offensive linemen want a quarterback involved in their drills to call out cadence, as well as call plays in an active drill against the defense, should it be appropriate to do so.

All of these factors can be important. As such, all of them should be worked on every day. For example, it can be very helpful for the quarterbacks to take at least five minutes every day and time-up the run game with the running backs. This effort can be invaluable, given that the running backs get to work on their assignments, first steps, landmarks, and aiming points. It is also a great opportunity for the quarterback to practice his fundamentals of handing off or pitching the ball on an option.

Working with the running backs can also be a great time to run through any run-game checks to make sure that everyone is on the same page. Furthermore, it is an occasion during which any trick plays that might be included in the offensive game plan for that particular week could be practiced, if they involve the running backs.

The first steps of the quarterback are critical. As such, this period can be a great time to emphasize fakes by the quarterback.

Since there are usually more running backs on a team than quarterbacks, the quarterbacks can get a little winded if the tempo is good, and the fakes are carried out in a championship manner. If the quarterback gets winded, this is a time to emphasize the importance of the little things and the effort involved in a quarterback becoming a great faker. A quarterback should take great pride in being an exceptional faker. This attribute can help win ballgames.

As a rule, it doesn't take too long to buzz through timing-up the run game, if the tempo is crisp. It is also a good time to work on a few routes with the running backs. In that regard, emphasizing a particular route on a given day can be a good idea, particularly if any new or unusual route has been incorporated into the game plan for that week. The point to remember is that timing up with the backs is a must, and as such, it needs to be addressed on a daily basis.

As previously noted, it is a must for teams to work on individual routes to the receivers every day. By the same token, it is also essential to make sure that the tight ends don't get neglected in these group drills. It is very important in a well-rounded passing attack that the tight ends are a major component of the passing game.

The best passing attacks always seem to have a group of tight ends who catch at least 50 balls during the course of a season. When the tight ends and running backs are highly involved in the passing game, the defense is forced to defend the entire field. Every zone must be accounted for and covered. With all the zone pressures that are currently in vogue in the game, the tight end can be a major weapon if he's used properly. As such, it is more than appropriate to work (in rapid-fire fashion) on most every route the tight end might have for a particular week on air. It may be necessary for this work to be performed during pre- or post-practice. Regardless of when it is undertaken, the key point to remember is that the quarterback should throw to his tight ends on a daily basis.

In addition to individual routes on air, there are times during the week, when the quarterbacks and wide receivers will work against the defensive backs. It could be a screen drill; it could be 1-on-1, it could be any emphasis of the week. When the receivers go 1-on-1 versus the defensive backs, it is a great time for both the quarterback and the receiver to see how the quarterback must and can control the timing of the passing game.

When receivers get pressed at the line of scrimmage, each receiver has to have a strong sense of urgency to get off the line and into his route. It is during this group work that the receivers start to understand that the quarterback will throw the ball when he is ready. Accordingly, the receiver, who gets jammed at the line or takes too long to get into his route, simply won't get to catch the ball on that rep.

As such, the quarterback should be taught to throw the ball when he is ready, and if a receiver isn't where he is supposed to be, to throw the ball where the receiver should be. This routine should also be the case on any busted route by the receiver. A receiver should never be rewarded by catching a ball, when he has run the wrong route. As a rule, it typically doesn't take too many times of the receiver not getting to catch a ball to make him understand the sense of urgency that is required by the quarterback, as well as the passing game, in general.

Pass skeleton or 7-on-7 is a group drill that is done by almost every team on a daily basis. In fact, it has been discussed extensively throughout this book. This drill offers an excellent opportunity, for a team to work on the timing of both its passing game and all of the routes in the game plan for that week against the various coverages it expects to encounter. It is also a good exercise for everyone to get on the same page with regard to the necessary orchestration and proper spacing that are required to have an exceptional passing attack.

The drill is also a convenient time for the quarterback to practice his pre-snap procedure of looking at linebacker, safety, and corner locations in order to better help him know what coverage he is about to face. As discussed previously, the offense should complete an extremely high percentage of these throws, because there aren't any bodies in front of the quarterback or defenders coming after the quarterback to disrupt his timing or vision.

On occasion, a hiccup will occur during the week when the percentage of passes completed isn't as high as it should be. For the most part, however, the offense should complete at least 85 to 90 percent of its passes during pass skeleton work. If the offense isn't completing a very high percentage of passes against the defense on a consistent basis, a problem exists. One of the problems that sometimes occurs with pass skeleton work is that the quarterback becomes too comfortable, because down deep, he knows that no one is coming after him. As such, he always has a clear vision of the field.

It is important to note that team pass periods and team blitz periods should be incorporated into practice every day to make practice for the quarterback as realistic as possible. In reality, pass skeleton work can be an excellent teaching tool for the quarterback coach. For example, it provides a viable opportunity to see and coach the timing of when the ball should be thrown against the different coverages. Watching this drill on tape also enables the coaching staff to review the choreography of the passing game, the spacing of the receivers, and the footwork of the quarterback.

Another group drill—half skeleton—is a nice variation of 7-on-7. In this drill, the offense puts half of a formation on the field, while the defense takes half of a coverage unit. The two units then go against each other. This exercise is another viable way to teach the offense the proper spacing that is required on each different play. It is also a good method for getting numerous rapid-fire reps for both sides of the ball. As such, it is simply an excellent drill, in general, for teaching.

To maximize the number of reps performed, as well as to help ensure that players aren't standing around, the best way to do this drill is to have the offense start on a hash in a balanced formation. The running back should be included in the offensive unit, given that his presence enables the creation of a three-receiver side, i.e., the flood side. Hypothetically, if the ball is on the left hash, two receivers would go to the left, resulting in the defense putting its defenders to that side. Then, if it was predetermined that the running back would create the flood to the left or boundary side, he would line up on the left, as well.

At that point, the coach would simply either yell the play to everyone or signal to everyone, and then, the play would be run. As soon as the play is over, two more receivers, who should already be positioned to the right, can line up. The coach would then yell or signal a route to them.

The drill should be conducted at a really fast pace. In fact, a lot of good teaching should occur during this drill. The drill could also be modified to enhance the teaching opportunities. For example, the side to which the back goes, i.e., the flood side, could be changed. Furthermore, 3x1 formations could be employed by the offense and defended by the defense. In addition, because of the number of reps that can be executed during the drill, virtually every pass concept can be worked on and defended in a relatively short amount of time. Given the tempo of the drill, this period shouldn't last more than five minutes, in order to save the legs of the receivers for the rest of practice.

Another group drill that can help set the tempo for a great practice is the inside drill. This drill involves the offensive line, tight ends, running backs, and quarterback. On the defensive side, the defensive line, linebackers, and most usually a safety or two, are required. This drill is conducted on Tuesdays and Wednesdays, which are usually the most physical, as well as the two biggest, workdays of the week.

For the offense, every base run in its playbook should be called and executed. In a similar vein, for the defense, every base defense should be called and executed, as well. This is also a time for the offensive line to concentrate on their first steps and hat-and-hand placement. Furthermore, it is an opportunity for the offensive line to be physical and to try to dominate the line of scrimmage.

The same factor applies to the tight ends in this drill, as well. For the running backs, it is a time for them to focus on their first steps and landmarks. It is also a time for them to focus on ball security and hitting the hole. Furthermore, it is an opportunity for each running back to demonstrate a physicality about his game.

For the quarterback, it is a time to work on his checks, his first steps, and faking. If the drill is conducted in an appropriate manner, it should never last more than 10 minutes. Furthermore, both the first and second teams should work in the drill. Both the offense and the defense can benefit from this drill. All factors considered, the drill should set the tone for the intensity of the practice and the week of preparation. If the coaches can't "hear" the drill, then the drill isn't being done up to standard. In reality, pads should be popping on both sides of the ball. As such, in most circumstances, this drill should be very physical.

❑ Team drills. Personally, my two favorite team drills are team pass and team blitz. Team pass is a drill that involves 11-on-11. Obviously, most every call in the drill is a pass. A draw, a screen, or an option can and should be sprinkled in to keep the defense honest. As such, the drill provides a very feasible way to simulate game conditions. Accordingly, the exercise can be a beneficial drill for everyone, especially the quarterback.

The quarterback, for example, has the opportunity to throw with bodies coming after him. He also gets to see and work against coverage rotations and occasional blitzes. As such, he needs to focus on bearing down and going through his reads with poise, and still be mechanically sound. Furthermore, it is a great time to ensure that everyone is on the same page with their assignments and execution.

Team blitz is just like it sounds. On every snap, the defense is coming. This drill provides an opportunity to make sure that the offensive line and running back are sound in applying their rules of the particular protection that has been called. It also gives the receivers the chance to understand how the timing of the passing game can change in a fraction of a second, when all types of pressure are being applied to the quarterback.

The best factor about the drill is that it puts the quarterback under a very intense pressure cooker. As such, it is important for him to display the poise that is necessary to go through the proper reads and progressions. It is also essential for him to put to use all of the drill work that has been undertaken, regarding his movement in and around the pocket. Furthermore, it is a great time for him to work hard at sliding, as well as at shuffling to throw, when his vision has been impaired by an oncoming rusher.

Team blitz is as good a teaching tool that the quarterback coach has to coach the quarterback's pocket presence and pocket mobility. It is a drill that should be performed every day at practice, because of the sheer volume of defensive pressure that most teams apply. As a rule, teams that are serious about being formidable at throwing the football will devote at least 10 to 15 minutes a day to this drill.

CHAPTER 13
Quarterback 365

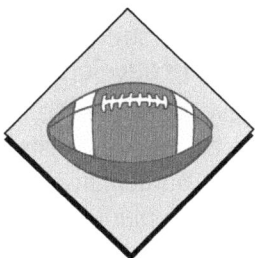

Developing into a championship quarterback is a year-round process. Most quarterbacks want to be coached. The great ones wake up every day, thinking about how they can improve.

Summertime

It can be argued that summertime is one of the best times for quarterbacks to work on their skills and techniques. The weather is warm, and the sun is usually shining. Fall camp is just around the corner, and it's getting close to time to play football.

As such, there are four parts to the quarterback's summer that are critical to his overall development, including the following:
- Weight room
- Speed, agility, and conditioning
- Mechanics and throwing regimen
- Film study

❏ Weight room. It is important to realize that muscular fitness plays a big part in the development of a quarterback. As such, the summer months are a great time for the quarterback to get bigger, faster, and stronger. When starting a summer strength training workout regimen, the quarterback should initially assess and determine how much he can lift on all of his exercises. This evaluation will provide him with a clear indication of where he is and will also aid in helping him set viable goals for the improvement he intends to achieve from his strength training efforts. As a rule, this undertaking usually entails an 8- to 12-week program, one that emphasizes the basic core lifts of the bench press, the squat, and the power clean. These lifts address all of the large muscle groups of the body.

When performing these lifts, it is essential that the quarterback closely adhere to the proper form and technique for each exercise. Such an approach will help maximize the gains he achieves from his training regimen. It will also help to keep him from being injured in the weight room.

Other outcomes are also extremely important for the quarterback to focus on, while he's engaged in his summer strength program, including core, shoulders, groin, and neck areas, as well as the development of better balance.

Core exercises are imperative because the core is integral to the quarterback's overall physical development, as well as instrumental when he's throwing the football. Weighted core exercises, particularly that involve the oblique muscles that use chopping motions that cross the plane of the body develop the muscle groups that are used when the quarterback is throwing the football.

In correlation with the upper-body lifts, a shoulder pre-hab program is designed to strengthen the small muscle groups and ligaments surrounding the rotator cuff. A pre-hab program, using bands, is a proven way for the quarterback to develop his shoulder strength and to prevent injuries to this part of his body.

Among the exercises that can be done with bands are front raises, 45-degree raises, and 90-degree raises. Bands can also be employed to perform external rotation and internal rotation exercises that isolate the rotator cuff. On the external rotation exercise the resistance is to the inside of the body. The elbow, which should be at a 90-degree angle, and the humorous are stationary. The internal rotation involves the same movement only with the resistance generated from an external location. Given that the quarterback will take thousands of drops during his career, the groin area is another key area that must be maintained, strengthened, and developed.

Inexplicably, a number of individuals overlook how important it is for the quarterback to have a strong neck. It is critical that the quarterback work to get his neck stronger, because stronger necks help reduce concussions. This fact has been widely documented by anecdotal evidence collected concerning quarterbacks from all over the country, who miss playing time because of a concussion.

Some quarterbacks who have suffered a concussion miss a week or two, while others miss an entire season. In fact, a few notable NFL quarterbacks have had their careers cut short, because of the number of concussions they have experienced over the course of their playing career.

It is essential to be aware of the fact that most concussions don't occur because of a blow to the quarterback's head by a defender. Rather, most concussions result from the whiplash effect of being hit in the head and the instability of the neck muscles to slow down the backlash. For example, this factor can be observed when the quarterback hits the ground, after being tackled, and his head bounces off the turf. In reality, the quarterback, who works hard on his neck strength, is better able to control the amount of whiplash, thus making the threat of a concussion much less.

It should be noted that the point is not being made that some quarterbacks who have suffered a concussion didn't work on their neck or have a strong neck. It does, however, indicate that the stronger the quarterback's neck is, the likelihood of him getting a concussion is reduced.

One-leg squats are a great exercise to strengthen the lower body, as well as help enhance better balance in the quarterback. While it is important for the quarterback to have great strength in his push-off leg for his throwing motion, it is also essential that his other leg be just as strong. Given that this leg is the one that is most exposed to oncoming rushers, it must be just as strong as the push-off leg. One-leg plyometrics are another way to help improve the quarterback's level of explosiveness and balance.

❏ Speed, agility, and conditioning. This period is also the time of the year that speed and agility training is most often implemented. As such, speed and agility work are an integral part of the quarterback's summer. Since most of this training is undertaken with his teammates, it is a great opportunity for the quarterback to exhibit his leadership skills. Everyone should see the quarterback show up for every single workout. Every teammate should see the quarterback striving to finish first in whatever drill is being performed. The quarterback needs to be fully aware of the fact that his actions are a reflection of his commitment to excellence. By giving 100 percent at every training session, he is exhibiting a mental and physical toughness that all of his teammates will respect and appreciate. The point to remember is that working in the weight room is a great time for the quarterback to become the unquestioned leader of the football team.

Summertime is when the strength and conditioning coach works to get the team in condition to play football games. As a rule, this effort encompasses several components, including working on speed, agility, stamina, and flexibility. For the quarterback, one of the most beneficial parts of this training is speed work.

Speed work for the quarterback could involve a variety of elements, for example, starts, 20-yard sprints, 40-yard sprints, or 60-yard sprints. It should be the goal of every player, not just the quarterback, to get faster. As such, the quarterback should devote one day of the week to sprinting every week of the summer. In reality, the only way to really get faster is to run fast.

The next day of the quarterback's summer training regimen should entail some sort of conditioning work. This effort could involve a number of elements. For example, initially, he could be required to perform 10 100-yard sprints or five 200-yard sprints. Every week, the reps he does should increase, building to a max of sprinting 2000 yards cumulatively per training session by the end of the summer.

The third day of the quarterback's summer workout schedule should be devoted to doing flexibility exercises, which could entail strictly performing stretching exercises or taking a Pilates class. This day is valuable, because not only is the quarterback resting his legs, he is also becoming more flexible in the process.

The next day should consist of engaging in some sort of lateral movements. In that regard, agility drills of all kinds could be incorporated. These types of quick-twitch movements are designed to improve the quarterback's overall level of quickness and lateral movement. The following day should be devoted to another conditioning workout.

After the running is over on a particular conditioning day, these periods provide the quarterback with the opportunity to then go through a series of three-step and five-step drops. His play-action footwork should also be worked on, as well. Doing these drops at this particular time is good, because the quarterback is fatigued, which should simulate what he might feel like late in the fourth quarter of a ballgame or during an overtime period. The sixth day should be another day devoted to stretching.

In summary, a summer running regimen should consist of one day of sprints and two days of conditioning, with position-specific drills, followed by one day of agility drills and two days of flexibility work. Just like most everything in our world, weight training and speed training are always evolving. The point to remember is that a number of different ways to train exist. If a quarterback is dedicated to getting better and works hard at it, he can get bigger, faster, and stronger. His underlying goal, whatever training regimen he ultimately adopts, is to be in tip-top shape for football season.

❑ Mechanics and throwing regimen. The summers have always been the best time for the quarterback to work on his mechanics. More often than not, he can work on a mechanical flaw during the summer and come back to fall camp, with his deficiency eradicated. In general, warming-up is one of the best times for the quarterback to work on any mechanical issue he might have. During this period, he can take his time, implement a particular drill that targets his problem area, using it as a warm-up, and make significant progress in addressing his defect.

During the summer it is imperative to institute organized throwing drills. The month of May, for example, can be a good time to have organized 7-on-7 sessions, twice weekly. In addition, the quarterback should work on his footwork in both the running and passing games.

The quarterback should also spend at least 10 minutes with the running backs during every organized workout to sharpen his ability to hand off or pitch the ball to them. It is also a good opportunity, during that particular 10 minutes, for him to throw to the backs to help them with their pass-catching and route-running skills. It is also a good time for the running backs to understand how important they are to the overall development of a great passing attack.

After spending time with the backs, it is a good idea to throw individual routes to the wide receivers for 10 to 15 minutes. They can either work on every route in the playbook or can emphasize two or three specific routes for that specific segment. After that session, the quarterback can work with the wide receivers in a 1-on-1 period against the defensive backs for another 10- to 15-minute segment. The throwing session should end with a 7-on-7 period against the linebackers and defensive backs for another 30 minutes or so.

On numerous occasions, the coaches can't be out on the field organizing and coaching. As a result, it usually falls on the quarterback's shoulders to recruit, organize, and lead these throwing sessions. This situation is another example of how a quarterback can enhance his leadership skills and position on the team.

Every month that goes by, another throwing session day should be added. In June, the number of throwing workouts should be upped to three times a week. By July, everyone should get together four times a week. If the quarterback coach has done a good job of teaching the proper mechanics of throwing the football, there shouldn't be too much concern regarding the quarterback developing a sore arm or overthrowing. Rather, the primary focus, at this point, should be to break up the sessions and make sure that the players have some fun with them.

While it is important for the passing game to start to take shape in the summer months, it is also essential that the throwing workouts don't become drudgery for the players. As such, a number of steps can be undertaken to incorporate a degree of fun into the sessions. For example, especially in late June or July, the players could switch roles. The offensive players could play defense, and the defense would be on offense for half of a 7-on-7 session. Another possibility might be to occasionally let a player on both sides of the ball play a different position for half of a session.

Such steps can help keep them interested and allow them to have some fun, while still having an opportunity to improve their skills over the course of the summer. In fact, many phenomenal passing attacks have started with a solid base that was developed in the hot summer months. While work certainly needs to be done, it doesn't need to be undertaken without some fun involved. The players should be excited to come to fall camp, and not worn down or burned out because the summer workouts were either too routine or too long.

The quarterback should be keenly aware of his fundamentals during the summer workouts. In that regard, he should be fully aware on every snap if all of his basic mechanics are sound. As such, if he is working on something during this time, it is important for him to keep the big picture in mind and worry more about improving than on completing a particular pass play. The completions will come in the fall, if his fundamentals and the mechanics are honed and improved in the summer.

The quarterback should always have a checks-and-balance system in place, if his coach can't be on the field with him during workouts. There should always be someone who is told what to look for, as he watches the quarterback go through his workout. This factor is very important, because it is in no one's interest if the quarterback develops bad habits, while the coach isn't with him. In a similar vein, the quarterback doesn't want to think he is getting better at a particular facet of his game, if he really isn't.

❏ Film study. Summers are a great time to start watching film of the upcoming season. Nothing gets a quarterback's mind on the season quicker than watching his upcoming opponents on film. As such, it's a great time to take the first opponent and break the film down, just like the quarterback would during the season. Furthermore, not only is it an excellent opportunity to get back in the swing of things with regard to breaking down film, it can also be a good way to get the quarterback excited to get going.

The quarterback can approach his film study in a number of ways. For example, he can take the first three games of the upcoming season, if tape is available on those teams. One game at a time, he can break down the film on those opponents.

It should be noted that even if his coach wants to handle the film study, it can be beneficial for the quarterback to allot several days out of his week to breaking down film on his own. The effort can be well worthwhile. For example, breaking down four teams would only involve a month of the quarterback's summer. While other factors can be watched, it can be really useful to include film of his upcoming opponents in the overall process of the summer film study.

Fall

The fall is the quintessential time of the year. Football season is why all the hard work was done all the rest of the year. All of the summer training has been completed, and now, it's time for football. Fall is broken up into two seasons—training camp and the regular season. Most teams are allowed 29 practice opportunities before their first game.

❏ Training camp. Camp is very important, because there are almost as many practices in camp as there are the whole rest of the season. Camp is a great time for many reasons. For example, there are no classes. There is no social calendar. It's football and more football, all day long.

The hours of training camp vary between teams. For most teams, the training camp day usually starts around 6:30 in the morning, with lights being turned off somewhere around 10:30 or 11:00 at night. Aside from all of the practice time, the time built into the schedule for meetings can be a great opportunity for the quarterback to get better. Having the quarterbacks in meetings for two to three hours a day can be priceless.

The first meeting with the quarterbacks is very important, because it can set the tone for the year. The rules and expectations are introduced at this meeting. This session is both individual and personal for the coach. It is essential that the coach makes sure that the quarterbacks understand that he will always be there for them, no matter what.

Each quarterback must be aware of the fact that his coach cares more about him than about his football ability. The quarterback must be comfortable talking to his coach about anything. There may be a number of things going on in the lives of these young men. For them, their coach has to and must be a place where they can go for advice or counsel, without feeling stupid, threatened, or alone.

Aside from the obvious factors, like being on time and being the first ones out to practice, as well as the last ones to leave, the quarterbacks need to understand that their position group will and must be the best and hardest working group on the team. Nothing short of championship effort, both in the meeting rooms and on the field, will be tolerated.

As a rule, three meetings a day are generally held during camp. Arguably, the best way to approach camp is to start with the very basics. It doesn't matter, if the player is a fifth-year senior or a true freshman, everyone should be coached like it's his first time. Anytime a quarterback coach takes it for granted that an older player knows something or should know something is a mistake. There usually isn't a year or training camp that goes by that something that should be known and completely understood by an older, more experienced player turns out that is hasn't been completely grasped.

The first meeting of each day is a great time to go over every play that is being installed for that particular practice. In that regard, coaches who have the technology can introduce each play with a cut-up of how the play should look. With all of the tools at the disposal of the coaching staff, the quarterback should never leave the meeting room without feeling totally prepared to execute.

The second meeting should consist of watching the previous practice, so that the quarterback can see what he did on the field—both the good and the bad. If a second practice is conducted on a day, plenty of time should be left to install and implement one or more plays for the next practice. If anything has to be cut short, it should be the film review from the first practice, because that can most usually be caught up with in the third meeting. If a second practice isn't held, most of the time in the meeting can be devoted to watching film.

The third meeting consists of watching film from the second practice or installing plays for the next day's practice. If there was no second practice, the installation of plays for the next day should occur. As previously discussed, it is very important for the quarterbacks to hear what plays will be worked on during the next practice.

The quarterback should be fully aware of the fact during training camp that he will be put in a variety of tough situations and won't be coddled throughout practice. It is essential for him to have the comfort level of knowing what is going to be called in practice, because this scenario is exactly what happens during game week. Going into a game, he better know what plays are going to be called, and, in what situations they are going to be called.

Night meetings can be a great time for a little quarterback bonding. If some time is left over, having the quarterbacks tell a little bit about themselves, or tell a joke, or talk a little about their girlfriend can be a great way to build a comfort level within the group. The quarterback coach should certainly not be immune to these jokes, stories, or whatever else that might come up.

Practice is fairly standard for most programs. Quarterbacks should hustle out to the field and start getting their arms loose. It is very important for them to properly warm up. It is also essential for each quarterback to make his warm-up partner give him a target.

Given that accuracy is at a premium, it's never a good idea for the quarterback to just go out and throw without a purpose. He should try to hit his targets on every throw. In fact, warming up like this can enhance his skill set. Who can hit the most targets? Starting out at 10 yards, throwing nice and easy, and then backing up every five throws is an effective way to warm up. During his warm-up, it can be desirable to have the quarterback simulate a few drops of all kinds and move a couple of throws on the run.

An effective way to end the quarterback's warm-up is to have him long toss a couple of balls. 35 or 40 yards is plenty, to help make sure that he is good and loose. It should be noted that some coaches like to implement drills into the warm-up for their quarterbacks. While, all factors considered, that's fine, it's never a good idea to sacrifice throwing to targets, because of the accuracy that can be learned, appreciated, and gained along the way.

More often than not, there is a 10- to 15-minute period of time where the quarterbacks are just by themselves during a particular practice. This period of time is typically when some aspect of the plays that are being installed that day are being worked on. For example, a different blitz look or blitz check may be undergoing a review. Whatever the case might be, this period is the best time for the quarterback to work on his footwork and mechanics.

Footwork and mechanics are the winning edge for the quarterback. Drops of all kinds should be practiced. Over and over, day after day, the quarterback who has the most consistent feet and most consistent drops has the best chance to end up being the most consistent passer. This period is usually the only time when the quarterback can exclusively devote to working and trying to perfect that aspect of his skillset. The rest of the day is typically spent on some sort of group or team work.

The next half hour or so is usually devoted to having the quarterbacks work with individual groups. In that regard, the running backs, tight ends, and wide receivers usually get a piece of the quarterback time during this period, which will be spent working on a particular play that might be installed that day or working on basic fundamentals, such as handoffs, pitching the ball on option plays, etc. It is also essential that the quarterbacks work, every day, with their wide receivers, throwing individual routes to perfect timing and chemistry. Everyone involved needs to understand that balls on the ground will not be tolerated. In order to have a championship passing attack, very few balls should hit the ground, no matter whose fault it is.

The next phase of a fall camp practice typically involves performing a pass skeleton or a 7-on-7 drill. The duration of these drills typically varies, depending on the philosophy of the head coach. After these drills have been conducted, it's usually time to go against the defense. The quarterback should understand that no matter what drill is being done or what group work or team work is going on, his underlying objective is to be flawless in every aspect of his game. From his on-the-ball procedure, to his checks, fakes, pre-snap reads, progressions, thought-processes, body language, and mechanics, perfection is his goal. As such, every quarterback must be coached on every play. Period.

Scrimmages are a major component of fall camp. Among coaches, differing philosophies exist concerning how many scrimmages to have during this time, because of the chance of a season-ending injury occurring to a player, particularly to the quarterback. Regardless of the number of scrimmages that are held during camp, it is important to make the scrimmage as game-like as possible for the quarterback, from a preparation standpoint.

Most coaches don't allow their starting quarterback to get hit during any practice or scrimmage. Given this being the case, it's extremely important to try and simulate the mental aspect of the game, as much as possible, which means having a game plan and going over it in detail before the scrimmage. The quarterback should know what to expect what play will be called on first and second down, as well as what to expect in every third-down situation.

Every situation that is to be scrimmaged should be prepared for by the coaches and discussed between themselves and their quarterbacks. From an evaluation standpoint, scrimmages are huge for the coach and the quarterback. On any number of occasions, starting and backup quarterback roles are finalized as the result of the fall camp scrimmages.

As a consequence, it is very important and very fair for all the quarterbacks in the group to understand what the offensive plan is going into each scrimmage. In fact, everything but getting hit should be simulated. The final scrimmage is a good time to put together a mock game, which includes having every situation possible occur. Everything, from injury timeouts, to equipment problems, onside kicks, a kick after a safety, two-point plays, last plays of the game, and overtime procedures should be rehearsed. The quarterback should feel confident leaving the scrimmage that there is nothing that he will face that hasn't been shown to him or practiced, which should give him great confidence going into that first game.

Not only is camp long, it can also be grueling. As such, it is particularly important for the quarterback to take care of his body, which means getting plenty of sleep, drinking fluids like crazy, and icing his shoulder and elbow after every practice. The attitude toward icing has evolved over the years. Previously, no one ever iced his arm. Now, everyone seems to be doing it. Since camp is a relatively long time, especially if there are multiple practices in a day, it's a good idea to ice. As discussed previously, I have never been overly concerned with "pitch counts." Times will occur during camp, however, when it makes sense to schedule a special teams emphasis day, during which the starting quarterback would be held out of 7-on-7 drills, as well as any other throwing that might be involved. A day of emphasizing special teams is a good practice or time to rest the arm of the starting quarterback. It's also a good day to let the other quarterbacks experience getting the majority of the reps.

❏ Regular season. Once the season begins, and game week rolls around, all of the players have a mandatory day off. On this day, the quarterbacks come in on their own and study film. This is a great opportunity for the quarterback to get many of his questions answered on his film study breakdown sheet that was previously covered in detail. This is often a time when a championship quarterback is somewhat like a kid at Christmas, as he hustles in the football office, asking to watch film. This day spent watching film will give him a huge head start, going into his position meeting on the upcoming Tuesday.

In general, colleges designate Tuesdays and Wednesdays as their big work days of game week. On these days, the practices tend to run around two hours in length, which makes them the two longest practice days of the week. As a rule, the general game plan is typically installed on Tuesdays. It is also the primary day to practice in full pads. All neutral down calls are installed and practiced. The offense practices against all base defensive fronts and coverages, as well as the defense's best blitzes. Wednesdays can either be with full pads again or with only shoulder pads and helmets on more situational days. On those days, third-down and red-zone plays are practiced against the defense's main fronts, coverages, and blitzes. When Thursday rolls around, it is usually either a shorts or a sweats-and-helmets day.

The entire offensive game plan should normally be practiced on Thursday. One viable option on Thursday, if field space is available, is to have the offense drive the field, coming out from the minus one-yard line and work all the way down the field for a touchdown and a two-point conversion. If undertaking such an option, all of the top calls on the call sheet should be utilized, which would be a great way to simulate the game as much as possible for one drive. As a rule, Fridays are used for walk-throughs and meetings.

Quarterback tips, reminders, and a test provide an effective way to start the Friday meeting. After reviewing the test and talking through the tip sheet, the quarterback may have questions that need to be addressed. This schedule still gives the coach ample time to deal with any issues that may exist and make sure that his quarterback is supremely confident going into the ballgame.

Friday night meetings are an appropriate time to watch film as a whole offensive unit. Cut-ups by formation are a good way to initiate this effort. It's also a good time to ask the quarterback, in front of the team, what his run and pass checks are against particular fronts and coverages. This scenario serves as a way for the entire unit to see one last time that their field general is on top of his game. Subsequently, in short two- to three-play bursts, the squad should watch how the opponent defends situational football, such as coming out, third down, red zone, goal line, and two-point play defense. All of the players, not just the quarterback, should leave the Friday night meeting, feeling like they could whip the world. Saturdays usually include a short meeting and then, it's time to go play.

Every ballgame is graded by most coaching staffs. A variety of different attitudes are held by coaching staffs concerning how or what they want to get out of a grading system. The system that works the best for me is one in which the quarterback either gets a plus or a minus. Did the quarterback get the job done?

In reality, a number of position coaches exist in football who will give an effort grade and a technique grade, as well as an assignment grade. Effort should never be an issue for the quarterback. Technique can be coached. On the other hand, if the quarterback misses an assignment, the chances of experiencing success on that play are about zero. Accordingly, the quarterback receives either a plus or a minus.

In the plus or minus system of grading, if a quarterback grades out at 92 percent, he has earned is a winning grade. Anything under 92 percent means that the quarterback didn't play as well as he was capable of playing, which made our chances for success as a team much more difficult.

Either on Sunday or Monday, depending on which day the team has off, is when the team should watch game film, typically as part of a position group. Furthermore, every play of the game is meticulously reviewed. Typically, the quarterback has already watched the film on his own. As a result, he should know what was done wrong before the play unfolds on the tape. These sessions can be a terrific learning opportunity for the quarterback. After a hard-fought win, in particular, these periods of watching film can provide a fun and enjoyable experience.

Winter

The winter months offer a great time for the quarterback to get better in a number of ways. There should be at least three focal points that should be worked on during these 8- to 12-week periods, including the following:
- Strength program
- Film study
- Throwing regimen

❏ Strength program. The winter workout program should look pretty much like the workout program of the summer, without the organized group and team throwing sessions. During this program, developing the major muscle groups of the body should be undertaken by performing the bench press, the squat, and the power clean. The winter is also an excellent opportunity to perform exercises for the core, shoulder pre hab, groin, and neck, as well as lifts that can help enhance the quarterback's level of balance. All of the lifts that were previously discussed in detail for the summer apply in the winter. As before, the quarterback should be tested to determine his existing strength level on various evaluative measures. Such testing will also allow him to set his training goals for the winter.

In most developmental training programs, during late January and early February, a series of winter conditioning drills is usually performed. These drills, which some coaches refer to as "mat drills," are a series of agility drills, designed to push the athlete to his max, both mentally and physically. As a rule, the drills are done in short bursts, with high intensity and very little rest.

This situation provides another opportunity for the quarterback to assert his leadership by finishing at or near the top at every station. For everyone to see their quarterback, not only push through but compete to win at every station, can be an eye-opener to his teammates. His efforts also can help to secure his place as a leader. These "mat drills" are undertaken in conjunction with the weight program in the winter. In reality, a number of individuals believe that this is where the toughness of the individual, as well as the toughness of the team, is rooted.

❏ Film study. The winter months can also provide an exceptional opportunity for the quarterback to improve himself by studying film. With the current technology that exists, there isn't much that a quarterback can't study. During this period, he can watch game-by-game mechanics and decisions, and situational football, as well as study the quarterbacks on other teams. It is a great time for the quarterback to really be honest and objective about how he played.

Watching film offers a viable opportunity for the quarterback to really learn the game, inside and out. The ability to watch all the factors that were done well, both mentally and physically, as well as all of the things that weren't, can help a quarterback grow immeasurably. Furthermore, if the quarterback learns to keep things in proper perspective (i.e., lose his unduly large ego, if he has one), a great opportunity exists for him to improve significantly.

Ideally, the program the quarterback is a part of will be able to afford these types of next-generation computer editing systems that make it relatively easy to undertake the in-depth analysis of film that will maximize the amount of information that is available to him. Regardless, he needs to watch everything that he can get his hands on that his coach has that can help him improve.

The winter months provide the quarterback with a viable opportunity to go through every play of every game he played in over the course of the just completed season and break it down, particularly the passes. It is essential that every play be analyzed as thoroughly as possible. As such, he needs to note not only if a ball was complete or incomplete, but why. The following checklist details what the quarterback should look for on every pass play:

Physically/Mechanics
- Was there a wide base?
- Weight back?
- Short step?
- Step slightly to the left of his target?
- Release point?
- "Z" in his lead leg?
- Follow-through?

Mentally
Pre-snap:
- Coverage?
- Blitz keys?

Post-snap:
- Coverage?
- Eyes looking where they are supposed to be?
- Correct read? Why?
- Result?

It is essential that the quarterback is very critical of his mechanics, while he is studying himself. The benefits of such an approach can be substantial. For example, he will be able to see why a throw was missed about 98 percent of the time, just by looking at the aforementioned listed mechanics. As such, he needs to understand that if a certain mechanical deficiency keeps showing itself on tape, that factor must be a point of emphasis when he throws to his receivers.

It is also important that the quarterback study what the pre-snap coverage looked like, and whether any blitz indicators existed before the snap. Studying this information at this point can help him tremendously in the fall, when he's watching film of opponents during the week. The quarterback should be very hard on himself, when looking at all of his key indicators. He should be especially hard on himself when viewing his head on tape to see if his eyes were really where they were supposed to be.

A quarterback who is not locked in to what he is supposed to be looking at is a quarterback who is figuratively just floating along in outer space. The likelihood of positive things happening when a quarterback isn't locked into where his eyes should be or on his movement keys aren't very good. The great quarterbacks put their eyes where they are supposed to be and then go through their progression.

After all of the aforementioned factors are viewed, it can be relatively easy to determine why a play was successful or not. In reality, a play can still be successful even if multiple players on offense don't do what they are supposed to do, but the quarterback does exactly what the play was designed for him to do. On the other hand, on occasion, everyone can do the right thing but the quarterback and the same play may have very little chance of success. In reality, however, a quarterback who is sound can make all of the difference between winning and losing. More often than not, this difference-making capability is the result of the detailed film study that he undertook during the winter months.

After watching each game, the next step for the quarterback is to watch cut-ups and situational football. Examples of cut-ups include specific plays, interceptions, touchdown passes, sacks, completions and incompletions, etc. Examples of situational football include third-downs, red zone, coming out, etc. The ability to watch a certain factor over and over again, while time-consuming, can be a productive way for the quarterback to better understand and grow his game.

Once the quarterback understands how to study film, it is relatively easy for him to watch and learn how the greats in the game play the position of quarterback. Most quarterbacks generally love to watch as much NFL film as possible, given that they fully enjoy sitting and viewing some of their boyhood idols in action. To a degree, doing so provides them with an opportunity to hypothetically play coach and be able to critique the mechanics and decisions of the best quarterbacks in the game.

❏ Throwing regimen. Throwing twice a week this time of year should be encouraged. As such, such efforts usually involve throwing to individual receivers, as opposed to a full group. Throwing twice a week during this time period should be sufficient for the quarterback, particularly if he is devoting an appropriate amount of time and effort in the weight room and the film room.

This period is also a good time to get a feel for any new receivers in the program, as well as an excellent opportunity to work on the chemistry between the quarterback and receivers who are already in the program. Organized pass skeleton and group drills aren't a necessity at this time, because the focus should be on the individual. This effort will also help condition the quarterback to be able to transition into undertaking additional throwing sessions each week, as team activities and spring practice approach.

It is essential that the quarterback understands that the winter months provide a meaningful opportunity for his teammates to see how hard he is working at his craft. As such, during this period, the quarterback should establish himself as someone who will lay it on the line every day. In other words, the quarterback should realize that no matter what the lift is and no matter what the drill is, he should strive to be and do the best every time.

Furthermore, if the situation involves some sort of agility drill or a team run, the championship quarterback should always strive to finish first. Nothing gains the respect or the attention of a group of players more than to see their quarterback win most every competitive activity. The winter months, which are the farthest months away from the start of football season, can be a great time for the quarterback to make himself the unquestioned leader of the team, because of the work ethic he displays day in and day out.

Spring

The spring can really be broken down into two primary elements: the couple of weeks leading up to spring practice and then spring practice itself. Most strength coaches want the athletes with whom they are working to remain in the winter strength program as long as possible before spring practice in order to maximize their strength gains.

❏ The couple of weeks leading up to spring practice. In reality, the only change in the couple of weeks leading up to spring practice should be the quarterbacks organizing a couple of 7-on-7 throwing sessions per week, which can get them their timing back, as well as knock the rust off of the passing game. These sessions can provide a great way for players on both sides of the ball to start to get the feeling that practice is just around the corner.

Strength testing of the players, including the quarterbacks, can be conducted during the week leading up to spring practice to determine how much strength has been gained by each athlete during the winter program. The quarterback should also be very focused in analyzing the degree to which his goals for the off-season program were successful. In addition to the throwing sessions, the quarterback should go back and review the cut-ups of the offense and have everything fresh in his mind, just before the start of spring practice.

❏ Spring practice. Once practice starts, spring football for the established quarterback and for quarterbacks fighting to move up the depth chart look very much different. For the established quarterback, it is a time for him to really concentrate on the fundamentals and mechanics of the positon. It is also a time for him to focus on the little things. As a rule, the established quarterback won't get the number of reps that he does in the fall. In reality, a number of his reps will be given to younger or more inexperienced players. His knowledge of the offense should allow for helping the younger quarterbacks to improve, both in the film room and on the practice field.

On the other hand, some quarterbacks will be trying to make a push for playing time, while the fundamentals and mechanics for them will be major considerations, what will also be important is the fact that reps will be at a premium. Because quality reps are invaluable, every day is big for the quarterback who is fighting for playing time.

The spring is no different than the fall for the coach who is trying to make sure every quarterback is prepared for every play of every practice. The results of scrimmages are a major factor in determining the depth chart for the fall. Accordingly, every quarterback must be prepared to play his best every time out.

During every scrimmage, the coach should simulate a game as much as possible for the quarterbacks. In that regard, there should be a call sheet that is reviewed, and every situation studied. Every quarterback should have the same opportunity to be successful by his efforts to prepare for a scrimmage. The coach should try and make it as "fall-like" as possible, by the amount of attention to detail and the level of intensity with which the scrimmages are conducted. An important component for the quarterback is to be able to take the grease-board aspect of the game and translate it to the field. Also, the ability to handle the intensity and pressure of the situation is important for the coach to be able to witness because some quarterbacks wilt when the lights start shining the brightest.

Spring football can be a relatively fun time. Typically, it is often more physical than the fall for at least two reasons: because coaches aren't quite as worried about injuries, and because there are usually many positions up for grabs. As a rule, the starting quarterback never gets hit during spring ball, except in games. For the quarterbacks who are trying to establish themselves, however, this stipulation isn't always the case. In a number of instances, especially in close races for the backup job of quarterbacking, coaches will allow them to be hit. This philosophy allows the coach to fully see how a quarterback plays when they are "live." In reality, a few quarterbacks exist who play very well when they know that they aren't going to be hit. Once the bullets start flying, however, their level of production goes down dramatically.

In most cases, quarterbacks like to be live. Quick whistles by coaches and officials are often a significant source of aggravation to most quarterbacks who get "sacked" and "tackled." Without exception, competitive quarterbacks love to really play.

There are a few quarterbacks, however, who like the security blanket of not being live. These quarterbacks are "coach-killers." They tend to look really good, until the "glass starts breaking." At that point, they become noticeably less effective. These quarterbacks will never reach their full potential, simply because they are lacking a huge necessary ingredient for being a championship quarterback—courage.

The spring is a short season because most strength coaches want to maximize both winter and summer strength programs. Whether a program starts spring practice early or late in the spring, the running and lifting programs revert immediately to full force. The spring is a time for coaches to evaluate their players. It is also a period when the quarterbacks can improve their level of physicality, as well as their overall knowledge of the offense and the game, in general.

For the championship quarterback, spring is a time to reinforce the fact that he is a great quarterback who is ready to perform at a championship level—right now. For the soon- to-be championship quarterback, it is a time to show everybody there is a player who is quickly rising through the ranks who will be a force with which to reckon.

Regardless of the time of year, it is important to remember that championship quarterbacks don't occur by accident. Rather, they are a by-product of coaching, training, and concerted effort.

ABOUT THE AUTHOR

John Bond is entering his 31st year as a college football coach. During that time, he has been a part of five conference and division championship teams and has been to five bowl games. He has four FCS playoff appearances to his credit at two different universities, including a #2 finish in 1999 at Illinois State. In 1999, Bond was a finalist for the American Football Coaches Association Assistant Coach of the Year Award and won the Mike Campbell Top Assistant Coach Award in 2003.

As an offensive coordinator, Bond has directed units that shattered virtually every existing offensive record at three different institutions at the time of his departure. In 2005, he was listed by Rivals.com as the eighth most impressive offensive coordinator in the country. At Illinois State, he coached quarterback Kevin Glenn, who is now eighth in the history of the CFL in passing yards with over 43,000 yards, as well as a sure bet to one day be a member of the CFL Hall of Fame. In 2005, he coached Phil Horvath, of Northern Illinois University, who was rated in several NCAA Division 1-A statistical categories, including being the only quarterback in the country that year to complete over 70 percent of his passes. At the present time, Bond serves as the offensive coordinator and quarterback coach at UT-Martin, where in 2015 he coached Jarod Neal, who finished in the top 10 in five statistical categories, including throwing for 3117 yards and 30 touchdowns.

John is married to the former Jenny Wilder. They have three children, Mackenzie, Mallory, and Brody.